PRESSED INTO MY PURPOSE

You Are God's Diamond, It's Time to Rise And Shine

PRAISE FOR "PRESSED INTO MY PURPOSE"

"This book is an easy read. It's full of insight on how to pursue, accomplish, and fulfill one's God-given PURPOSE, in spite of all life's uncertainties. Pressed into My Purpose encourages us to put God first, so that He can direct our path in our pursuit of PURPOSE."

- **Minister Hattie Broadnax**

"Wow! This is one of the most dynamic and encouraging books I have ever read. I wish that I could get one into the hands of every person struggling with self- worth. It really ministered to me."

- **Dr. Doretha Allen,**
President of Berean Light Institute

"Dr. Chatmon, I hope you continue to use the gifts that God has given you. Your words of inspiration will minister into someone's life who is in need. May you continue to listen to God's voice and be obedient to His Word. God bless you, and congratulations on your success."

- **Margaret T. Lee**

PRESSED INTO MY PURPOSE

You Are God's Diamond, It's Time to Rise And Shine

DR. LORRAINE CHATMON

PRESSED INTO MY PURPOSE
Copyright © 2015 Lorraine Chatmon

All rights reserved. No part of this book may be reproduced, distributed or transmitted in any form by any means, graphics, electronics, or mechanical, including photocopy, recording, taping, or by any information storage or retrieval system, without permission in writing from the publisher, except in the case of reprints in the context of reviews, quotes, or references.

Scripture quotations are from the Holy Bible, *English Standard Version*®, ESV®. Copyright © 2001 by Crossway, a publishing ministry of Good News Publishers. All rights reserved.

Published by: Purposely Created Publishing Group™
Printed in the United States of America

ISBN-10: 1-942838-29-8
ISBN-13: 978-1-942838-29-6

FOR INFORMATION AND ONLINE ORDERING CONTACT:
Dr. Lorraine Chatmon
www.LorraineChatmon.com
www.BeautifulRichLife.com

Special discounts are available on bulk quantity purchases by book clubs, associations and special interest groups.
For details email: sales@publishyourgift.com
or call (888) 949-6228.

For information logon to:
www.PublishYourGift.com

TABLE OF CONTENTS

Dedication	ix
Acknowledgements	xi
Foreword	xv
Introduction	xix
1 Dropped Out But Not Counted Out: The Pressing Begins	1
2 You Are the Potter of Your Purpose	15
3 Pain and Problems Pave the Way to Your Purpose	27
4 Your Destiny Will Not Be Revealed When You Are Distracted	41
5 Diamonds, Pearls, and Your Purpose	57
6 Free Will vs. God's Will	73
7 My Higher Calling	91
8 Answering Your Call and Serving with Purpose	107
9 Making Room for Your Purpose	125

TABLE OF CONTENTS

10 It's Time to Shine 145

Afterword 163

About the Author 175

In loving memory of my parents,
Richard and Mary Robinson,
and my siblings, Evelyn, Tommie and Richard Jr.
I love and miss you.

This book is dedicated to…..
Every soul, searching for their purpose and enduring
the press to become a shining diamond in the world.
You are God's diamond!

ACKNOWLEDGEMENTS

First and most importantly, I give thanks, honor and glory to my Heavenly Father for gifting me with the ability and courage to write this book. Secondly, I thank God for my husband, Oscar L. Chatmon, who has always been by my side, through the good times and bad, the rough roads and smooth paths that we have traveled for over forty years together. I thank him for his love, support and encouragement through all my ventures, and for giving me space, time and financial support to pursue my educational and career goals.

I want to send a special thank you to my children: my son, Antonio B. Robinson and his wife, Charlene; my daughter, Catina D. Shaw and her husband, Mel. Children are such a blessing, and I'm grateful for my son and daughter and the beautiful grandchildren they have given me. I love my grandchildren, Vonte, Antonio Jr., Lorraine, Merissa, Mark, Tymal, and Breanna, and my great-grandchildren, Tyshawn, Zion, and Anan'ese.

I wouldn't be the woman I am today without having such brave, warm and loving parents. Although they have passed on, they are still with me in my spirit. Thank you, Richard and Mary Robinson, my father and mother, for giving me the gift of life and teaching me that despite obstacles, I could be and do anything I dreamed of. Rest in heaven; I love and miss you. I'm also very grateful that my parents gave me friends for a lifetime in the form of brothers and sisters. Thank you, Christine, William, Hattie, Charles, Thelma, Gwendolyn, Priscilla, and Veronica. I love and appreciate you.

Family is the foundation for all that I do. Although I cannot mention all of you, I love and appreciate all of my nieces, nephews, cousins, aunts, and uncles who, in their own special way, have touched my heart and served a beautiful purpose in my life. Special thanks to my church family at New Life Christian Center and Antioch Missionary Baptist Church, my kingdom leaders, staff, and members of the congregation. Your trust in my leadership means the world to me, and I appreciate all of your love and support. I love you dearly.

No one makes it in life alone. All great accomplishments are achieved through the help of others. This book is a reality because of the love, support, and mentoring of some great people in my life. Thank you Rev. Gladys Robinson for being my confidant, I love you. Ruby Hatch, you mean the world to me, thanks for being my friend.

DR. LORRINE CHATMON

I so appreciate the mentoring, guidance, and support of Catrice M. Jackson, my book writing coach and message mentor. Thanks for lovingly pressing me to finish this book and for believing that it was possible. I appreciate you. Birthing my message was a challenge, and I am so excited my book is here for the world to experience. Tieshena Davis, thank you for all of your wisdom and expertise in helping me polish my book into one that I love and am proud to share with the world. I appreciate you.

FOREWORD

By Catrice M. Jackson

*"The soul which has no fixed purpose in life is lost;
To be everywhere, is to be nowhere."*
- Michel de Montaigne

If you take your last precious breath today, will you have lived on purpose? Are you living fearlessly and courageously? Do you wake up excited about life? Do you have a clear vision, and are you executing your destiny? Are you doing what you love, loving who you are, and serving the world with your greatest gifts? If not, you are a lost soul trying to be everywhere and going nowhere.

If you are not living on purpose, you are living by default. That's right, you are letting life happen to you instead of creating the life you desire.

If you are not walking in your purpose, you are walking in circles and maybe even in the dark. If you are not serving the world with purpose, you are not carrying out God's perfect plan and purpose for your life. This may be a hard pill to swallow, but it is the truth.

PRESSED INTO MY PURPOSE

Another truth is that you can start doing it all right now. Every breath you take is priceless, and every move you make should be with purposeful intent.

This is the moment you stop waiting for your dreams and desires to come true. Now is the time to take a front row seat in God's classroom, get your divine assignment, carry it out, and fulfill your destiny as it is designed. You are more powerful than you realize. Who you see yourself to be is just a shell of your true brilliance. You are so much more than your body, thoughts, feelings, and experiences. There are no tangible words to describe the true, perfect, and beautiful essence that you really are. You are so especially unique that only your creator knows the definition of who you are in the deepest core of your being. You are perfection. You are exactly who you are supposed to be. You are far greater than what you see in the mirror. You are magnificent. You are a divine soul on a hand-crafted journey designed *just for you* by God.

You have a profound purpose in this lifetime. You were born with it. It is within you, ready to be activated and shared with the world. You may not know what your purpose is or it may be a faint or foggy memory. You may have abandoned it or lost your way due to the demands and overwhelming moments in life, or you may have no memory of your purpose at all, but I want to assure you that your purpose is very much alive inside of you right now.

Perhaps you do know what your purpose is, but are unsure of how to embrace it and carry it out. Maybe you *know* who you are and what you are here to do, but you are afraid to take action towards living your purpose-driven life.

It doesn't matter what your circumstances are in this moment. If life has beaten you down, tested your faith, stunted your growth, or caused you to doubt your magnificence and significance, you are being pressed into *your* purpose. It's all a part of God's bigger plan for your life. Dr. Chatmon does a wonderful job, illustrating how what may seem to be too much or too difficult in your life, is just what you need to be cut into the diamond that you are.

Pressed Into My Purpose chronicles the life of Dr. Chatmon and how she transformed obstacles into opportunities, struggles into strength, and pain into purpose. Her courageous story and gems of wisdom shared in each chapter will challenge you to ponder your own purpose and push back when life presses you down. She, for the first time, reveals one of her greatest struggles and how she overcame the shame and stagnation it once created in her life.

Pressed into My Purpose takes you on a personal journey to rediscover your purpose, embrace it, own it, and live it powerfully. Prepare to be enlightened, encouraged, empowered, and equipped with the insight and tools you need to be gracefully pressed into your own purpose. This book urges you to not die with your purpose unlived and unfulfilled.

This is your moment to live on purpose and with a purpose. Now is YOUR time to live fearlessly and courageously. This is your moment to answer the divine call and carry out our unique purpose assignment in life. Get ready to create a clear vision, develop a purposeful plan, and use your divine spiritual gifts to be of great service to the world. Dr. Chatmon's heartfelt, honest story will inspire you to be who you are, love who you are, do what you love, and live a passionate purpose-led life.

"Destiny is a choice, despite your circumstances."

-Catrice M. Jackson,
Bestselling Author, Speaker and Brand Expert

INTRODUCTION

> *"A life without purpose is just a meaningless walk through life, but a life with purpose is a divine journey of the soul."*
> **– Dr. Lorraine Chatmon**

Greatness, life fulfillment, and success are never achieved without struggle. Just like the butterfly, you too will have to experience some constriction, darkness, pain, and struggle to eventually fly into your purpose, and no diamond would ever shine if it didn't endure the pressing and cutting required to be brilliant. You are already a butterfly and a diamond. Your beauty and brilliance already exist. It's up to you to say yes to the cocooning that is happening in your life, embrace it, and then courageously break free. It's up to you to say yes to the pressing and hold strong to your faith and belief that you *will* survive the cutting of life. All of the pain, struggle, and challenges you've faced or are facing now are preparation for your destiny. Every single moment of your life is preparing you and positioning you to walk confidently in your purpose.

There are so many people who wake up every day with no vision, no plan, and no intention for their life. They go through the day checking things off of their to-do-list and carrying out the same old routines in life. At the end of the day, they are tired, frustrated, exhausted, and unfulfilled, yet they wake up the very next day and do the same routine all over again. They don't get excited about life because their passion has been buried under blame, shame, and life challenges. Their dreams have faded into non-existence, and they have become a robot of redundancy, aimlessly moving about in the world. The sad and beautiful thing is they are the only ones with the remote control to either keep walking dead or move in the direction of something better, more fulfilling and liberating.

Are you on a meaningless walk in your life? Have you become a robot of redundancy? Have your life's challenges pressed down upon you to the extent that you don't press back? The butterfly doesn't become a butterfly by staying in the cocoon. It becomes a butterfly because it unleashes the courage to be released from the shell that holds it captive. It's not even capable of or meant to stay locked in the cocoon. The destiny of the caterpillar is to become a butterfly! Life may have you in a chokehold right now. Your challenges may be consuming you, and you may even be on an aimless walk in your life with no clear vision, plan, or purpose. If you are feeling the pressures of life and wondering when your breakthrough will come, this book is for you. I must warn you, however, that your breakthrough won't be handed to you. It won't show up at your door and say, *"I'm here to set you free."* You have got to unleash your courage to push back, press through, and break out of anything that is keeping you in bondage. Now is the time to set yourself free and shine in your purpose.

YOU are already God's diamond, my friend! The brilliance, beauty, and shine within you is waiting to be released. In order to fully embrace your shine, you must accept and embrace the press. The press is the pain, problems, challenges, obstacles, setbacks, failures, lost relationships, financial struggles, and every other experience in life that does not feel good. Through these moments, you truly discover the meaning and purpose of your life. When the "pressing" happens, it causes you to think deeply, reevaluate your priorities in life, make changes, and be shaped and molded into the person you are *meant* to be. If life were filled with mostly success and delight, you would never transform, grow, and evolve into your divine greatness.

The pressing is a *gift* from God. The pressing transforms you from an ordinary hunk of carbon to an extraordinary diamond. The pressing reveals the preciousness of who you already are in order to rediscover, reveal, and walk in your purpose!

God didn't make a mistake when He created you. He knew exactly what He was doing. He also knew that you'd need to be prepared for this purpose and what kind of pressing you would need to reveal your true, authentic beauty, brilliance, and shine. Whatever is happening to you or in your life is purposeful. Like a hunk of carbon buried deep beneath the earth's surface, you too are being cut, pressed, and shaped so you can fully emerge just like a diamond. Are you ready to break free from yourself? YOU are the only one holding yourself captive. It's time to shine. It's time for you to be *pressed into your purpose!*

Throughout the pages of *Pressed Into My Purpose*, I share real "pressing" moments in my life that almost derailed my dreams and kept me from living my purpose. I reveal a part of who I am that has never been shared publically with the world before. A part of me that kept me wallowing in shame and living in the shadows of my life for a long time. I share examples of how, when life pressed me too hard, I chose to press back instead of becoming paralyzed. I share these experiences to inspire you to be courageous and to empower you to press back against life's challenges, prevail personally, and shine in your purpose.

DR. LORRINE CHATMON

God has not forsaken you. In fact, He's at the end of the tunnel, waiting for you to emerge. He's ready to deliver you! He's endowed you with a vision, talents, gifts, and a passion that may be buried in the pressing of life. I hope this book inspires you to unleash the courage to set your purpose free by turning on your inner light so that you may be a light unto others who are cocooned in the chaos of life and burdened by the darkness of the press. You are God's diamond, and it's time for you to shine!

"God always gives us strength enough and sense enough, for everything that He wants us to do." – John Ruskin

Dr. Lorraine

CHAPTER 1

Dropped Out But Not Counted Out: The Pressing Begins

"We all make mistakes, have struggles, and even regret things in our past. But you are not your mistakes, you are not your struggles, and you are here NOW with the power to shape your day and your future."
- Steve Maraboli

I wasn't born with a silver spoon in my mouth, nor am I related to Rockefeller. As a matter of fact, I was born into a large family with very little money. However, we had a lot of love and respect for each other. My mom and dad taught us to love God, to love each other, and always be there for one another. My parents gave us the best life they could afford. They financially struggled to send us to school, so the thought of going to college was out of the question. I wanted more out of life, so I set a goal to one day earn my doctoral degree. Based on the socio-economic status of my birth family, getting an elementary school education was a privilege and a financial stretch, but deep down inside I knew getting higher education was a necessary part of my unknown purpose at the time.

Somewhere deep in my soul, although we were financially poor, I knew education would be a big part of my elevation into a greater purpose for my life. We *all* have a purpose in life, and I can recall when the pressing of mine began.

I remember sitting in a little, two-room classroom one autumn day. I believe I was in the second grade. I was wearing a cute (at least I thought so) hand-me-down dress with pink flowers all over it. I had to be very careful not to get the dress dirty or tear it because one of my other sisters might have to wear it the next day. Other girls in my class would verbally bully me because they didn't like the clothes I wore or the way I styled my hair. I had long, pretty hair, and my older sister always made sure it looked nice. She would add ribbons and bows to my ponytails, and I loved it. I just wanted to be like everyone else—to be accepted, and yet, I never understood why the other girls didn't like me. I was afraid of them.

When I was in elementary school, I had low self-esteem and felt like I wasn't as smart as the rest of my classmates. I didn't understand why I could not read well or solve math problems like everyone else. Often times in school, I was consumed with fear and would pray the teachers would not call on me to answer questions or solve problems in front of the class. There were many days my heart would beat really fast, my hands would sweat, and I would be overwhelmed with anxiety and fear. There were even days when I felt ashamed and humiliated by my peers for being different. The teasing and bullying got so bad that I wanted to drop out of school; yes, drop out in the second grade. Every day, for quite some time, I would get up in the morning, get ready for school, and instead of going to the bus stop, I would go and sit under the bridge not too far away from my house. I'd sit there alone and frustrated until it was time for the bus to come pick us up after school. I would walk home as if I had been in school all day, and my parents didn't know any different. I just couldn't bear going to school, being teased and feeling like I didn't fit in.

I continued sitting under the bridge for a long time, until one day I decided to stay at home in bed. I recall my mother asking me why I was not up getting ready for school, and I said, "I don't feel like it." She didn't probe much deeper than that, and she didn't make me go to school that day. This was the day I dropped out of school in the second grade. You may be wondering how it was possible for me to do that. Well, I'll tell you. First of all, my mother had twelve children, and I was number six and somewhat caught in the middle as I saw it. My mother and father worked very hard, had very little money, and the stress of raising twelve children was overwhelming. We barely had enough money to survive, let alone cover the expenses of everything. I guess she figured by allowing me to stay home, she'd have one less child to spend unavailable money on. I really don't know why she allowed me to drop out, but at the time, I didn't care because I got exactly what I wanted. So I thought...

I was too ashamed to tell my mom the real reasons for not wanting to go back to school because I knew it would deeply hurt her to know her baby girl was being bullied and humiliated by classmates. My mother loved and cherished her children, and to think that anyone would hurt any of us would have made her angry, and she wouldn't think twice about showing up at my school to handle the situation. I didn't have the courage to tell her that her baby girl was embarrassed and ashamed for feeling I wasn't good enough, so I allowed my feelings to dictate my decision. I was just a child and did not know the depth and cost of my choice. I just wanted to feel better, and in my young mind, dropping out was my only way to escape.

Those of us who were raised up in the South during the 50s knew that dropping out of school was no big deal or surprise to many folks. Education was not a high priority during that time. Many families needed the children to stay home and work on the farms to help feed the family and generate income. Some of my brothers dropped out of school to work on other people's farms. We, of course, did not own a farm, but my dad raised livestock and grew a garden to feed our family. Even while attending school, there were times we needed to stay home to help my father with chores. My mom had her hands full, taking care of our needs by cooking and taking care of the house, and my older sisters were needed to stay home to babysit some of us. Unfortunately, many parents in that era didn't have the opportunity to go to school themselves because of similar circumstances. My father, for example, completed the sixth grade, and my mother completed high school; this was considered an accomplishment during this time, as many parents didn't go that far in school.

I had missed so many days of school, hiding out, that I wouldn't have passed to the third grade anyway. That same year, my neighborhood friends were excited about their grades and that they would be third graders the following year. Many of them asked, "Lorraine, are you planning to return to school next year?" I tried so hard to be excited for them; however, my feelings of failure and shame overpowered any joy

I had inside for them. There was a part of me that was jealous of their success and excitement, and although I was physically free from the fear and anxiety of having to go, I secretly really wanted to be in school.

I thought I would at least be able to find joy in the upcoming summer break, and quite honestly, I was looking forward to not having to think about school, grades, or deal with any of my classmates. Well, my summer break was not as enjoyable as I thought it would be. The consequences of my choices were really starting to sink in, but, by the time summer break had ended, I managed to pull myself together. As I reflect back on how young I was at the time, I realize how very wise I was, too. God spoke to me in ways that a young girl could understand. Something inside of me let me know that I was good enough and that everything was going to be alright, so I decided to give myself permission to be who I was and accept myself, flaws and all. I remember reading a scripture in the Bible that said, *"We are uniquely and wonderfully made."* Knowing that bit of truth gave me the courage and strength I needed to walk in the classroom with confidence, knowing that I could excel if I put forth my best effort. It was not uncommon for me to read the Bible at an early age because we were raised in the church and encouraged to read God's word. I'm so grateful for that upbringing because that one scripture gave me the courage and confidence to go back to school.

When I returned to school in the fall of that same year, I knew I would have to repeat second grade. It was bittersweet, but it gave me an advantage. The schoolwork was easier, and I was able to excel in my subjects with more confidence. The best part was the bullies from last year were now third graders, so I didn't have to deal with them. I also was the older and wiser student in my class, and many of my classmates looked up to me. I made a lot of great friends and really enjoyed second grade that time around. I did it! I passed the second grade with my newfound self-confidence.

What's most exciting about all of this is, at the time, I did not know that I had dyslexia. I didn't find that out until later in my life, but one of main reasons I struggled in school was because I was often confused by what I would read and see on the chalkboard. All those years I thought I was dumb, different, and unable to learn, but the truth is, I had a developmental reading disorder that does not allow the brain to properly recognize and process certain symbols. Dyslexia creates challenges for those who have it, as it is difficult for them to comprehend written words. I'll share more about this and my journey in overcoming those challenges throughout the rest of the chapters. Shockingly, even with this disability, I was able to not only complete second grade, but graduate from the sixth grade.

I felt very optimistic and confident at the beginning of the next school year. I was going to be in the seventh grade, and that meant that I would transfer to a new school. It almost seemed as if my dyslexia had essentially gone away after I repeated the second grade. Yet, when I started the seventh grade, it appeared again in full force. It was the most challenging year for me. Dyslexia had become an ongoing irritant in my life. It seemed as if it had taken on a power I could not control. I was more frustrated, my thoughts were scattered, and my brain felt like it was in control of me instead of me being in control. Everything was becoming a blur, and I couldn't understand what I read; it was as if the letters danced around on the paper to a melody that I could not comprehend. Once again, I was overwhelmed and unable to focus or complete my assignments, and I was beginning to fall behind and fail my classes.

Dyslexia had totally consumed my mind, body, and spirit. I felt paralyzed. I didn't know how to tell anyone about what I was experiencing, nor did I know who to tell. It was almost as if there was a ticking time bomb inside of me, ready to explode any second. Once again, a spirit of fear and anxiety overtook my body. I feared being judged, labeled, stereotyped, teased, and bullied again. I didn't want to be seen as a slow learner or dumb. I didn't want to be seen as the girl with beauty and no brains. I also didn't know what to do about it, so there I was feeling hopeless and discouraged again. My grade point average and my self-esteem were falling lower and lower each day, and I started to withdraw from others and hide my feelings. One thing was for sure. I refused to drop out again. That voice within reminded me that I was here for a reason, no matter what I was experiencing at the time. I didn't know exactly what to do, but I knew I had to do something.

I was afraid to tell my mother about what I was experiencing. Going to the doctor was an uncommon practice in the 1960s, especially for people of color. Very few people in our low-income neighborhood could afford to go to the doctor. My mother was the type of mother who was very resourceful, creating home remedies for whatever sicknesses we encountered as children. I didn't want to burden my mother with my problems, and I also didn't want to create financial stress by requesting to go to the doctor, but I knew I needed more than mom's home remedy. So, instead of speaking up, I suffered through my pain and pressed my way through the seventh grade, barely making it, but I made it through. I started to ask for help from the teachers and my friends, and they were all so kind to help. But I called on my biggest helper, God, and began praying for healing from this mysterious disorder.

My mother used to always say prayer changes things, and I believed her, so I prayed to God every day to heal me from whatever was inflicting so much pain in my life and affecting my ability to learn and be successful in school. My parents weren't big churchgoers. Thank God for the neighborhood church mother, who would gather all the kids who wanted to go to church and take them with her. Even at a young age, I knew I was going to need God to help me overcome my challenges, so I gladly went to church and Bible study with the neighborhood church mother as often as I could. Between her and my sister, I learned about God and His miraculous power.

One particular day, while at Bible study, we were studying a scripture that essentially says "as a man thinks, so he is." I had one of the biggest revelations and aha moments of my life. I realized I was allowing my disability to define who I was and that I needed to think differently about who I was because I was *not* my disability. That moment forever changed my life. I kept pressing on in faith, trusting that God was going to fix my problem and that everything would be okay.

⌘ *Reflecting On My Purpose*

One of my core beliefs is that God is almighty and powerful. I now reflect and realize I am open to ask for His assistance and guidance for my every need. I believe I have the seed of greatness and purpose within me. I find extreme comfort and fulfillment when I talk to God. I ask Him to help me to overcome the obstacles that make my life unbearable and to unleash the things that keep me bound. My elementary school days taught me to persevere through the pain, and how that pain can serve as a point of purpose in our lives. I also learned to think my way into becoming who I wanted to become. I learned that my voice has power and to own it and speak into existence that which I desire. I learned to trust in God's word and to let go of the struggle by refusing to allow my pain to pave the way of my destiny.

I may have dropped out, but one thing is for sure, I was not counted out. God has a purpose for my life and yours, too. Living out your purpose is an inside job.

"What we achieve inwardly will change outer reality."
- Plutarch

⌘ Time To Ponder Your Purpose

Reflecting back on your early childhood moments, did you experience any pain or challenges that may serve as pressing moments that can help you pinpoint your purpose in life?

_____

_____

_____

_____

_____

_____

_____

_____

_____

_____

_____

_____

CHAPTER 2

You Are the Potter of Your Purpose

"If you always put limits on everything you do, physical or anything else, it will spread into your work and into your life. There are no limits. There are only plateaus, and you must not stay there, you must go beyond them." - Bruce Lee

Maybe you are wondering why I kept "pressing" in the direction of my purpose. Even in the seventh grade, I was wise beyond my chronological age. Instinctively, I knew I was putting limits on my life by allowing dyslexia and the challenges I had in school determine my destiny, and, as a feisty-spirited young woman, I refused to quit. I refused to allow my circumstances to overshadow my gifts and inner joy. I kept pressing on because when your purpose speaks to you, you must listen even when the message is not crystal clear. Like the *Little Engine That Could*, a voice within (and I know it was God's voice) whispered over and over again, "Keep going, and don't give up!" I knew

PRESSED INTO MY PURPOSE

God would not steer me in the wrong direction, so I trusted Him and said yes to seeing and living beyond my limits.

Problems, challenges, and pain are a part of our purpose. In many cases, people will tell you how they turned their personal pain into their life purpose. For example, someone who was abused as a child grows up to become an adult with a mission to protect children. They become child welfare workers, social workers, therapists, and advocates against child abuse. They turn what once hurt or hindered them into a cause they champion relentlessly. Others may choose to dig deeper than the problems and pain to discover a hidden treasure within by discovering talents and spiritual gifts that will help them shine the light on their capabilities instead of their disabilities.

We go through things in life to test our faith, to show us how strong we are, to ignite what we are unknowingly passionate about, and to share a testimony for others who may be going through what we've gone through. The only way that our test can become a testimony and our personal mess into a message is by facing our problems, pain, and challenges head on and digging deep within to discover our talents to be shared with the world.

I had to face my pain, my challenge, my truth. Yes, I have dyslexia, but it doesn't have me. Dyslexia is sort of an invisible problem. When I was in school, my teachers could see how hard I worked to complete my assignments, but they could not see all the steps it took in my brain to just make sense of the words I was reading. Eventually, I could figure out what I was reading, but dyslexia has a way of slowing down the connection between what you see and what your mind comprehends. Fortunately, thanks to recent research, there is a lot of scientific proof that a dyslexic person's brain is normal and healthy. Assistive technology, such as Scribe Smart Pens, Dragon Naturally Speaking Software, audio books, and CDs offer new ways to help those with dyslexia save time and overcome some of their comprehension challenges. I learned to conquer my challenges by learning how to be more observant, increasing my listening skills, and mastering the art of memorization. I was determined to not let dyslexia rule my life, keep me from excelling in school and life, or paralyze my purpose for living.

Perhaps you too are struggling with some kind of personal challenge, or as some call it a disability. I don't like the word disability because it implies that you are NOT able or that your challenge does not allow you to do certain things. I guess there is a kernel of truth in that belief, but only if you choose to live with that type of mindset. Your challenge doesn't necessarily have to be an official diagnosis either. You could be challenged by living with a spirit of fear, having low self-esteem, or just believing that your life doesn't have any meaning. While your challenges may be different, the truth is the same: You can overcome them; you can be brave and victorious; you can rediscover your gifts and talents and walk boldly in your purpose for being here. I did it, and I am not the only one with dyslexia who has chosen to defy personal challenges to live on purpose.

I am part of an eclectic community of brave souls who unleashed their gifts and talents and found their purpose in the world. Did you know that Robin Williams, Harry Belafonte, Jim Carrey, Danny Glover, Cher, John Lennon, Whoopi Goldberg, Pablo Picasso, Jay Leno, and Henry Winkler all have dyslexia? Each and every one them are successful in their own right and have made a big impact in the world. They chose to not let their "disability" *dis-able* them from being who they are, operating in their genius and living out their purpose for being here. You and I can do the same thing. We must because our lives have just as much significance as theirs. You and I were created to do something special in the world that only we can do, but it's a choice. You can either allow the pressing of your pain to paralyze your life or you can turn your pain into a purpose that you are passionate about. It's up to you. Maybe this story will inspire you.

As I searched the Internet for current research on dyslexia, I found the most amazing story shared by a man named Ronald D. Davis. I was inspired by it and thought I would share a piece of his "Behind the Red Dirt and Water" story with you.

> *Davis said when he was an infant, his mother told him he was a "Kenner's baby." A doctor named Leo Kenner coined the word autism in the U.S. Davis said for the first nine years of his life, he was oblivious to everything. He was aware that he was alive.*
>
> *During his first 11 years, he had to go school. He spent most of his time in the back of the classroom, sitting in a corner, facing the wall. At age 12, he said he still had not learned a thing in school. Not even the alphabet. His mother worked with him everyday trying to teach him the alphabet song. He said he could only learn a few letters.*
>
> *According to Davis, his brothers were normal, so they were allowed to have things and do things that were forbidden to him. They had watches and pocket knives. One night, Davis said he managed*

PRESSED INTO MY PURPOSE

to get one of his brother's knives and nearly cut off one of his fingers, he didn't care he still he wanted a pocket knife.

Somewhere in the void of autism, he discovered that by mixing dirt in the backyard and water together in a puddle, he could make thick goo. This substance could be formed into anything he wanted. The dirt in the backyard was gummy red clay, and upon letting it dry completely, it would hold its shape for a long time. He had no idea how many pocket knives, he made from red dirt and water. His brother's wristwatches were made of mental and leather. His was made from red dirt and string, but at least he had one.

When Davis turned 12, he said he was labeled "uneducable and mentally retarded." For him, it meant that he didn't have to sit in the corner anymore. He got to turn around and see what everyone else saw. In the meantime, while sitting in the corner, he noticed along one wall, just below the ceiling, a banner displaying the letters of the alphabet. He didn't know why he began copying them in the red clay and water. It took him awhile, but eventually he got each one made. Then he managed to put them in order, and asked his brother what they were. He would continue to *point at the letters and his brother would name them. He would play for hours on end with his clay letters.*

If anyone asked him to say the alphabet, he would just rattle off the letters at random, but not in order. People wanted him to say them in order, so for some reason he began with the letter "Z." Davis said it took him more than twenty years to learn to say the alphabet in the right order.

When he was 12, his mother told him he had the intelligence of a chimpanzee. At age 17, his intelligence was tested and he scored 137 points on the IQ test, which is above average. He eventually participated in speech therapy, and while he began learning how to speak, he still could not read. He remembers being told at the age of 18 that he would never learn how to read, write, or spell like normal people.

Davis' speech continued to improve, and each day, words became the focus of his universe. He then began to have ideas, and he would create his ideas in the form of clay. He named the ideas and between the ages of 17 and 27, he had created more than a thousand ideas and words modeled in clay. By the time he was 27, his IQ score had risen to 169. Davis went on to develop procedures to help people with dyslexia by using clay, which was very natural for him. Researchers soon discovered that other people with dyslexia loved working with clay and used it as learning tool, as well.

In conclusion, Davis believes the potential for genius in some form exists in all of us, if only we have a foundation on which to build our thinking, and a goal we desire to achieve. ("The Story Behind our Use of Clay to Model Words and Ideas" by Ronald D. Davis, from: the Dyslexic Reader, Issue No. 10 summer 1997.)

Like Mr. Davis, I kept pressing on no matter what. He has an amazing story, however, it's not an uncommon story to many people who have to deal with ridicule, shaming, bullying, and being labeled as disabled, incompetent, retarded, or unintelligent. You might look at Davis' story and feel his pain or pity his situation, but I encourage you to see the purpose for his life instead. Maybe Davis's situation is exactly how it was supposed to be. Maybe his autism is a gift which allowed him to develop possibilities for other people with autism to learn how to read and express their ideas.

There's a lot to learn from his story. You can choose to sit in your pain, stare at a blank wall, and be paralyzed, or you can choose to unleash your genius within and use your talents and gifts to change the world and live a fulfilling life.

Bible scriptures tell us that we are fearfully and wonderfully made. We arrived in life with God-given unique gifts and talents. God also gave us the gift of free will, which means we can do whatever we want. Unfortunately, it's often our own free will that causes us more pain and struggle than is necessary. We can diminish that pain and struggle when we listen to God's instructions on what we are here to do in the world. God has already created the perfect plan and purpose for us. If you focus too much on your "disability," you'll never fully walk in your ability to live a purposeful and satisfying life.

If you've been wallowing in your pain, feeling paralyzed by pity or putting your potential on pause, it's time for you to get out of that captivating corner you've been sitting in and get up and activate your purpose in life. You are a genius. You have special talents and gifts, and you are here to do something only you can do in the world. Your purpose has been perfectly prepared for you. Now it's up to you to use your free will to become the potter in your own life. What may look like a mess of dirt and water in your life is really a gift.

PRESSED INTO MY PURPOSE

Find the courage to mix that mess into a message and turn your pain into possibility, passion, and purpose. Don't let the "pressing" in your life hinder your purpose.

⌘ *Reflecting On My Purpose*

When I look back on my childhood, I once sat in the corner of pity. One day, I found the courage within to turn around and see that my life had meaning and I had a purpose, so I chose to pick up what I thought were broken pieces and mold them into a meaningful message for my life. God has not forsaken me.

My dyslexia is not a dis-ability. I am able, capable, intelligent, and genius in my own right. I have dyslexia, but it does not have power over me. I have become the potter of my purpose, and you can become your own, too. I dare you to unleash the power of your purpose today.

> *"It is not because things are difficult that we do not dare; it is because we do not dare that they are difficult."*
> - **Unknown**

⌘ *Time To Ponder Your Purpose*

What labels have you put on yourself or allowed others to give you that keep you from living up to your full potential? How can you become the potter of your life by turning your mess into a message?

_____

_____

_____

_____

_____

_____

_____

_____

_____

_____

_____

_____

CHAPTER 3

Pain and Problems Pave the Way to Your Purpose

"You can accept reality, or you can persist in your purpose until reality accepts you." – Robert Brault

Often times, your purpose is staring you in the face, waiting for you to say yes. Are you observing the reality of your life and only seeing the pain and problems, but have difficulty seeing the potential in your problems? Life's challenges and problems are simply lessons you must learn in preparation to live out your purpose. Nothing is happening "to you"; challenges occur "for you." In other words, when you begin to look at your challenges as opportunities, you'll realize that everything happening in your life serves a purpose for you to discover and activate your destiny.

Ultimately, you can change your reality by accepting and persisting in your purpose because when you live "on purpose," your reality becomes what you desire. It's always your choice. You can either accept the reality you see right now, including all the pain, problems, and challenges, or you can extract the purpose out of it. Whichever one you choose, you get exactly what you want. So what do you really want?

Maybe you are going through a transition right now. You desire something different and better in your life, but you have yet to experience it. Maybe you feel like you are in a long dark tunnel and can't seem to see the light at the end. This transitional moment is also paving the way into your purpose for living. If you're like me, you don't like transitions, but they are simply passageways into the next level of our lives. They are a part of our divine journey. If you are in transition now, I encourage you to see it as a bridge to get you from where you are to where you desire to be and to enjoy the scenery, embrace it, and learn valuable lessons along the way. It will all make sense in the end. I promise you. One particular powerful transitional time in my life changed everything and guided me one step closer to discovering and walking in my purpose.

Moving from Emporia, Virginia to Washington, DC with my sister, Christine, was a defining moment in my life. She was the first to leave the nest, and by doing so she opened the door of opportunity for many of us, especially me. Her departure had great impact on our family because, as the oldest daughter, she took on a lot of responsibilities in our home. She was a significant help to our parents, serving as a caregiver, teacher, mentor and, in my eyes, a trendsetter. She invited me to come live with her and help care for her two children, which was a dream come true for me. Having been raised in the South, I had not experienced the excitement of living in a big city. My life in Emporia was the only life I knew, but I also knew I needed to leave the nest to experience something greater than I could ever imagine. I quickly packed my bags and left the city limits of Emporia, Virginia for the first time to begin a new chapter in my life.

Upon arriving in Washington, DC, I must admit it was an extreme culture shock. I was used to living in the rural south on a farm with lots of trees and single-family houses. For the first time, I experienced apartment living and while I was excited, it was a challenging transition. Mind you, I was only 14 years old at the time. There were buildings everywhere with a ridiculous amount of traffic, people and noise. It was a bit scary, but I knew I made the right decision to leave the nest. It was one of the best decisions I ever made in my lifetime. For the first time, I experienced what is meant by the saying "bright lights and big city." I had never seen so many lanes filled with overflowing traffic, people moving and walking around everywhere, and it seemed as if everyone was always in a hurry. This was what they call the fast life, for sure. While I felt like a stranger in this new land, I was mesmerized by it all. Don't get me wrong. I loved Emporia, which is a beautiful place and a great city to start a family and raise children, yet I craved something more adventurous in life, and life in Washington, DC was certainly feeding my appetite for adventure.

I had always been told that Northerners were not friendly people who did not care about their neighbors. But I was also taught that if you want a friend, you must show yourself friendly. I started to adjust quite well to my new surroundings during the summertime and began making friends quickly on the block we lived on. I sure had some good times on Belmont Street. Later that fall, it was time for me to enter into the 8th grade. I attended a school named Frances Jr. High, where I finally developed a love for school. I loved the fact that I got a fresh new start. I didn't have to prove anything to anyone and my concern with dyslexia seemed to be minuscule to what these big city kids were facing. Besides, it appeared as is if many of my peers were more concerned with how they looked instead of getting good grades. I loved my school, I fit in, had lots of friends, and was not ashamed about who I was, and was actually getting good grades without struggle. Once I started excelling in school, I began to develop a passion for learning and education. According to Christine, education was the ticket to success. As my role model, she was right. Education meant a lot to her, and she made it her business to instill a love for learning and education within me. Truth be told, I was a willing student of hers. She was so smart and successful, and I wanted to be like her.

When I was 16, I met my "first love." He was handsome, charming, and quite irresistible. He sat behind me in one of my classes and would play with my hair every day. He finally had the courage one day to ask me if we could go on a date. He was hard to resist, so I said yes. We spent a lot of time together and officially became a couple. I was so smitten by him and enjoyed every minute we spent together. While I thought I had my priorities in order by putting school and education first, the day came where I failed to resist, and we eventually had sex. Unfortunately, I did not get enough education about sex and ended up getting pregnant. I was afraid and couldn't even begin to think about how I was going to tell my sister and parents. I was more afraid to tell my sister than I was my parents because I looked up to her and felt that I really let her down. I thought if I didn't say anything to anyone, the pregnancy would disappear. How naïve I was at that age to even believe that was possible. As time passed, I knew I had to tell someone because this little baby was growing inside of me, and I was growing on the outside. I found the courage to finally tell my sister and all hell broke loose.

She did not hesitate to tell me how disappointed she was. She talked down to me, yelled at me, and I'll never forget the words she said to me. She told me that I was no good and that I would never be somebody in life because I got pregnant at 16. Her words hurt deeply and almost choked the life out of me. She was right, so I thought at the time. Sometimes, even today, I can still feel the sting of her words in my spirit. She had high hopes for me and wanted me to live a successful life, and I ruined that by getting pregnant. I was ashamed, scared, and confused about what to do next. I didn't know the first thing about being a mother, and, in this case, a single mother. Once the irresistible guy found out I was pregnant, he was nowhere to be found. I was stuck all alone to raise this baby by myself. I really did feel alone because I felt like my sister had given up on me, but deep inside I knew she still loved me.

A few months passed, and I was still just as scared and confused. I didn't know what my future would be like.

All kinds of thoughts entered my mind. I contemplated an abortion, but was too afraid to go through with it. I knew my mother would not approve of me having an abortion. After all, she was a woman who birthed 12 children. I also worried that something might be wrong with my baby when it was born. I had so many racing thoughts that I felt like I was driving myself crazy. I decided it was time to tell my parents about the pregnancy, and to my surprise, they were not as angry as I thought they would be. They took it much better than my sister did. My mother asked if I wanted to come back home to Virginia, and I said no. The only way I was going to go back to the South was if my sister decided to kick me out, and thank God she didn't. Although she was very angry with me, she allowed me to stay with her and she helped me out through my pregnancy.

Nine months later, on January 14, 1969, I went into labor and experienced the most awful pain of my life for 10 hours. I clearly remember feeling terrified when two doctors came into my room and told me I was going to have to undergo surgery to have my baby. I wondered how it could get any worse, but I knew I had no choice but to say yes. A couple of hours later, I awoke out of a fog to see my eight pound beautiful son for the first time, whom I named Antonio B. Robinson. I thought I knew what love was when I started dating his father, but the love I had for my son was so deep, words cannot describe it. My life was no longer my own. This little baby depended on me, and I had to grow up fast to become a great provider for him. Being a teenage mother was not easy. I made a lot of sacrifices to create a good life for us and our journey included a lot of challenges. Some days I didn't know what to do or how we would make it through, but God always provided me with purpose and provision, and I'm proud to share that my son has grown into a handsome, responsible, loving, and extraordinary man who now has children of his own by his beautiful wife, Charlene. I love him dearly.

I thank God for my loving, caring, supportive family who came to my rescue by not abandoning me at a time I needed them most. You've heard it takes a village to raise a child, and my village helped me raise my baby and provide us with food, shelter, and clothing when I was not able to do so on my own. The stinging words shared by my sister inspired me to prove her and the world wrong. Instead of becoming a statistic, I finished high school and landed my first job with the Peace Corps two days later at the age of 18. My new job was another defining moment in my life. My role was to process the volunteer applications of those who were going to third world countries to teach survival skills to the native people. For the first time, I thought about the importance of being of service to others, particularly those less fortunate than me. At one point, I was inspired to become a volunteer myself to serve in Africa. Unfortunately, I never made the trip to Africa.

Eight years later, my son and I moved back to Virginia. I worked hard and saved money to restart my life back in my hometown. My sister is a retired accountant, and one of the greatest lessons she taught me at an early age was to save money, even if it was just a dollar at a time. She also taught me to not live paycheck to paycheck. I'm so glad to have her as a mentor because I wouldn't be the woman I am today without her love, guidance, teaching, and support. I've always wanted to make her proud because she invested in me and sacrificed a lot to help me live a great life. She never let her past dictate her future and was the first to leave home, the first to go to college, and the first to successfully raise her two children by herself. I cannot imagine how my life would have turned out without her love and guidance. She truly is a woman who turned her pain into possibilities and actively created her life.

Michael E. Gerber says, *"The difference between great people and everyone else is that great people create their lives actively, while everyone else is created by their lives, passively waiting to see where life takes them next. The difference between the two is the difference between living fully and just existing."* I made the choice when I got pregnant with my son to not exist but to live fully. I had dreams of going to college, obtaining a career, and owning my own home, and I refused to allow motherhood to cause me to live a mediocre life. I wanted the American Dream, and I believed my son and I deserved it. I wasn't exactly clear on what my American Dream would look like, but I was determined to be a role model for my son, give him the greatest life possible, and live out the destiny for my life.

The transitional moments I shared with you were all a part of the press, the shaping and molding of what I know today as my purpose. While I was going through the tunnel, it seemed as if I would never see the light. I didn't know it at the time, but the path to my purpose was being paved in every single pain and problem I experienced. There's no such thing as perfection. If you are expecting your life to be perfect before you step into your purpose, you are committing self-abuse. You are traumatizing yourself by expecting something that will never happen. Your message in the world will take shape right in the middle of your mess. The tests you are experiencing right now will become the testimony you share with the world. The pain and problems that may be consuming you right now are stepping stones paving the way to your purpose for living.

Your life means something. There is a higher calling for you to answer. You don't have to wait until the storm passes. The point of your purpose is being revealed to you in the chaotic moments of your life. You are not an accident and it is not a coincidence that you are here. God created you on purpose with a special purpose in mind. When you face trials and troubles, you have the opportunity to extract the essence of why you exist and what you are here to do. What's also important for you to understand is that your purpose will never be, or look, the same as anyone else's.

Your purpose may not be a big grand act. You may not be a world leader or celebrity; maybe your purpose is to be a loving and nurturing mother, supportive counselor, compassionate teacher, the next great inventor, the parent you never had, or motivational speaker. Every purpose has significance, including yours, so don't compare your path and purpose to anyone else, unless you are willing to experience the pain and problems they went through to uncover that purpose.

PRESSED INTO MY PURPOSE

Pause for a moment right now to intentionally see the potential and purpose in your problems. The challenges you are facing are the lessons of life's classroom and are preparing you to unlock and live your purpose. Everything that's happening is happening to shape and mold you into the diamond that you are. You can choose to feel pity about your problems, or you can turn your problems into possibilities that will activate your purpose.

Transitions are teaching moments. God is the master teacher and He uses trials, tribulations, and transitions to test and teach you how to advance to the next level. Stop perceiving your problems as your ultimate reality. Your problems can only paralyze you if you choose to allow them to. You are bigger and more powerful than your circumstances. Use the moments of chaos to activate your creative problem solving skills. Don't resist or run away from the drama, embrace it and courageously say yes to your purpose.

⌘ *Reflecting On My Purpose*

There were so many times in my young life when I felt overwhelmed by my problems and paralyzed by my pain. I wanted to give up and quit. Yet instinctively, I knew that everything was happening for me instead of to me. I didn't always have the answers or know what to do, but I knew my purpose was unfolding before my eyes.

In the painful and problematic moments of my life, especially as a single mother, I found the courage to keep the faith and say yes to my unknown purpose. I knew there was more to be discovered, even in the middle of the so-called mess. Don't let your circumstances dictate the direction of your destiny.

"Our background and circumstances may have influenced who we are, but we are responsible for who we become."
- ***Barbara Geraci***

⌘ Time To Ponder Your Purpose

Look closely at your problems—what are they pointing you towards? How can you take control and be creative in your chaotic moments? What possibilities have you missed because you are too focused on the pain?

_____

_____

_____

_____

_____

_____

_____

_____

_____

_____

_____

CHAPTER 4

Your Destiny Will Not Be Revealed When You Are Distracted

"For we are God's workmanship, created in Christ Jesus to do good works, which God prepared in advance for us to do." - Ephesians 2:10

I woke up one morning in August of 1979 to the phone ringing and ringing. I jumped out of bed and ran into the kitchen to answer it. When I picked up the phone, a voice on the line said, "Good morning, Mrs. Chatmon. We've been trying to reach you all week to interview for our position as our Senior Center Director. Can you come in for an interview tomorrow?" Of course, I said yes because I desperately needed a job to pay my college tuition. I was so excited to finally generate some income and return to school. And then I woke up. No doubt it was all a dream because at the time I didn't even have a phone installed in my home.

PRESSED INTO MY PURPOSE

There I sat on the edge of my bed disappointed because the moment felt *so* real. After about an hour or two, I could still feel the residue of the dream in my spirit. I just couldn't accept that it was all a dream. I felt cheated and a bit angry, too.

As I sat there wishing it were real, I distinctively heard a soft voice say, *"Call Mrs. Smith. She wants to talk you about a job."* I said to myself, *what job?* The voice said, *"The job in your dream."* I instantly knew it was the voice of God, a divine revelation, and I didn't hesitate to obey His command.

I did not want to miss my blessing, so I ran next door to my sister-in-law's house to call Mrs. Smith who had recommended me for the Senior Director position awhile back. She and I worked together at a day care center, which I had recently resigned from. She had such a beautiful spirit and was always looking out for me. Eager and excited, I called Mrs. Smith and found out she had been looking for me all week to tell me about the open position. I did indeed get the job and was so thankful for Mrs. Smith's support and referral. I needed this job badly, as I had recently enrolled in college and had no idea how I was going to pay my tuition.

My dream was truly divine intervention. I am certain of it. When God reveals Himself to us, it's up to us to be aware and pay attention to all the ways He speaks to us. He opened a door that I may not have been able to open myself. Do you know when God is speaking to you? Can you hear His voice? People often tell me they don't always know when God is speaking to them. I can relate, as sometimes it's not always clear to me when God is speaking. However, the dream I had felt so real. Have you ever had that kind of dream? The dream I speak of is one of those moments when you have to just trust that it is God's way of communicating with you. Often times, we dream of things that are buried deep in our subconscious mind, where our hopes, dreams, and soul desires live. God knew that I needed and wanted this job, but because I was so distracted by various personal challenges, God knew that I may not have heard His voice unless He spoke to me in a dream. I heard Him loud and clear and did not hesitate to take action.

When God speaks to you (and He always does), you may not hear His voice in ways that you expect. I think many people believe they will hear God's voice as if it is being broadcasted through a loud speaker or as if He is sitting right next to you having a conversation. His voice can certainly show up that way, but often He will speak to you in ways in which you are open, willing, and able to receive His message. Think about it. Could you really handle God speaking to you through a bullhorn? Would you be able to really receive His message as if He was sitting next to you or would you be afraid? God knows your heart and He knows what you can tolerate, even when you don't know. He knows whether you are easily distracted by life or sensitive to being overwhelmed. God knows your level of trust, faith, belief, and skepticism, so He will speak to you in the most effective way for you to *hear* his message.

Let's keep it real! Many of us say we are believers, but deep down inside we don't *truly* believe that God can do all the things He says He can do. We read our Bibles, quote scriptures, pray, and yet we still doubt God. He knows this about us. And while we may not intend to offend God by our lack of trust and belief, we do. So God knows exactly how to get His message to you in a way that you will not only hear it, but believe it and take action. Do you believe that God has forgotten you? Are you having trouble hearing His voice? Are you asking God to reveal the purpose for your life, but failing to hear His response?

These are very common questions for believers and especially those eagerly seeking clarification of their purpose for living. I'll admit that I, too, have these questions and feel unclear sometimes, but here's what I know to be true about how God speaks to us about

His purpose for our lives. Distractions drown out the voice of God. When we are distracted by problems, pain, issues, and challenges, we automatically adjust the channel in which God speaks to us, making it fuzzy and full of static—much like a radio station. When you are distracted by life, you must be intentional to keep the channel between you and God open. You have to turn the dial back on the God station by slowing down, reading your Bible, and meditating on His word. When you get still, you can more clearly hear God speaking to you. Another issue is that you may believe your problem is too big or too small for God to be concerned. He already knows what your issue is, and often He will not respond to it until you invite Him in to be your chief problem solver. God does not want you to suffer in silence. He already knows what you are going through, so you might as well talk openly about it to Him. Lastly, expect to hear from God. Don't doubt your significance. God loves you, sees you, and knows your struggles. Increase your expectation that God will not only hear your desires, but that He will answer them quickly and clearly.

Look at all the ways that you are either easily distracted by life or sensitive to becoming overwhelmed. Those are indicators of how you may not be allowing the voice of God to speak to you. Get still, be quiet, ask God to talk you, and ask Him to speak to you in a way that you will hear Him, know it's His voice, and then be obedient. If you are not going to take action on God's guidance and commands, why ask Him for help? Maybe that's why you are not able to hear Him because He knows you won't move your feet. And maybe, just maybe, the chaos you might be experiencing in your life *is* God's way of speaking to you. He's trying to get your attention, and maybe the only way He can get your attention is to create storms so you will call on Him. It doesn't have to be this way. You don't have to wallow in chaos and pain just to hear God's voice. His voice can speak to you daily and minute by minute in a very peaceful and encouraging way, if you allow it to.

Be open to all the many ways God can, and will, speak to you. He may send His message through a dream like the one I had, a friend you trust, a complete stranger, a book, a movie, or a marvelous idea that seems to just drop in your spirit. His voice may show up as a whisper or gut feeling that you know just feels right, but, more often than not, God's message is subtle and gentle. It's more of a whisper than a shout. Remember God created you and He knows how you will hear His voice. Finally, I want to share with you that God's word—His message and His voice—should always generate feelings of trust, peace, calm, and knowing within your spirit. If you hear a voice or get a message that agitates you or stresses you out, it is NOT the voice of God. Remove the distractions in your life, get still and quiet, and invite God in to speak to you and then take action.

Because I took action on God's command through my dream, He did not just give me a job, He gave me an opportunity to serve mankind. This was for sure a divine assignment because we are all here to be of service, so God often sends us to places where we are most needed and places where we can use our natural gifts to serve others. At this particular time in my life, God made it clear that my assignment was to be of service to the elderly community. I wasn't sure how long my assignment would last, but I was obedient to the direction He sent me in. You've got to trust that everything is a part of your unique purpose and plan. I accepted the position and loved my job so much that I stayed there for forty years. *Yes! Forty years!* I thoroughly enjoyed caring for the elderly, delivering meals to the homebound and serving in a leadership capacity to foster compassion for the aging.

Don't take your dreams lightly. From the beginning of time, God has spoken to His people through dreams, and many of God's prophets did marvelous things and accomplished impossible feats because they listened to the voice of God in the form of a dream. The most important thing to remember is that God is always speaking to you, but it's up to you to summon His voice, hear it, receive it in the way He communicates, believe, and do your part. You might feel like you are waiting on God, but, in fact, He is waiting on you to hear and listen for His directions about your purpose in life.

My job at the Senior Center, without a doubt, was God's plan for my life. I now realize that it was more than a job. I was placed in a vineyard, a place to witness and be a servant to those in need. Working there was truly an amazing experience, and it was an honor to be among such great men and women of God, who referred to themselves as the Saints of Old. Though my role was a leader, I was blessed to be a student of their wisdom as well. What a reciprocal relationship of teaching and learning I experienced in my time there. They gave me wisdom, and I gave them a new hope for life. Isaiah 43:10 says *"You are my witness, declares the Lord, and servant whom I have chosen, that you may know and believe me and understand that I am he."* This scripture reminds me and affirms for me that God had a plan for my life and being involved in the Senior Center was a focal point in my purpose. I was created to specifically fulfill that role for a season.

DR. LORRAINE CHATMON

In 2012, my season as Senior Director came to an end. I resigned with much gratitude for the privilege to be of service to the elderly because my job never felt like work. I knew that God already had my next steps and new destination all mapped out. You see, ever since the age of 18, God has ordered my steps and shown great favor in my life. My first job at the Peace Corps seemed to just fall into my lap. My second job was a coordinator's position at a daycare center, and when I moved back to Virginia, I landed my third job as the senior director. Every one of these jobs, God designed just for me. They were all a part of the bigger plan and served as stepping stones to what would come next after my retirement. I didn't seek out these jobs, they found me (God's favor) because they were a part of my unique purpose.

Sometimes your plan is not God's plan. After I retired, I planned to travel the world and see all of the places I had dreamed of. I had experienced much of the East Coast states, had been to Canada and the Bahamas, and spent some time in California, Alaska, Hawaii, and many states in between. During my journey, God spoke to me and informed me that it was time for another assignment. I was again given the opportunity to work as a substitute teacher in my local community in Virginia. *Me? A teacher?* That was my initial response, especially since I had so many difficulties in school and struggled with dyslexia.

My life had come full circle. Here I was, working in the same system that had once intimidated me as a child. Amazingly, I am an excellent teacher and love every minute of it. What an assignment! I am mentoring children and young people who have learning disabilities such as autism and difficulties in math and reading. I know God is winking at me because those were the same challenges I faced in school. Words cannot fully express how grateful I am for this experience and how rewarding it is to help children who are just like me in many ways.

One day, there was a little girl, who reminded me so much of myself at that age, sitting in the back of the classroom. She was quite shy, and I often detected a look of confusion in her face. She was struggling to comprehend the math equations being taught for the day. All of the other kids had partners to work on their assignments with, but she was alone, so I decided to be her partner. As I approached her, I was thinking to myself, *"God please give me the right tools to help her."* He granted my request. We worked on the math problems, and she was able to get all the answers right. I could see a sparkle in her eyes. She felt so proud of herself and a bit of her true personality began to emerge. I knew I was in the right place, doing the right thing at the right time.

Sometimes you may feel that you've done all you can do, but God's purpose for your life is everlasting. Just when you think you've accomplished your purpose, He will find a way to re-purpose your life until it's time for you to leave this earth. My purpose has certainly been renewed, and I know there is more to come and more divine assignments to complete. What's also ironic about my season of teaching is that one of my colleagues is someone who bullied me when I was in the second grade. One day, she approached me and said, "Lorraine, please forgive me for bullying you all those years ago. I am ashamed of my behavior." She went on to say how she was jealous of me at the time for being skinny and having long beautiful hair. I accepted her apology, and we laughed about old times and made amends. *Isn't God wonderful?* He has an awesome way of working things out for our good. As a second grader, I thought I was being bullied because of my learning difficulties. Unfortunately, I was bullied just for being me.

Those days are long behind me. I am free from the bullies of the world and refuse to let other people treat me that way ever again. I know I am a child of God and that I am worthy of love, honor and respect. I was too young to understand it at the time, but now I know that everything I went through and experienced was preparing me for the assignment I am fulfilling today. I also know that season will come to an end and there will be a new assignment. I trust the plan God has for my life, and I continue to summon His voice, listen to it, and follow His lead. The voice of God is often what people call your intuition. That gut feeling inside or that hunch you get to do something or not to do it, that is God speaking to you.

Don't dismiss the power of your intuition. According to Ellie Drake, *"Intuition consists of genuine hunches and a calm knowing within. I now know that to live in fulfillment, I must honor my inner knowing of the direction my life should precede. I trust my ability to listen to my intuition and then acting upon it is the most essential part of fulfilling that destiny."* Ellie doesn't have any special power; she just listens and obeys the voice within. You have the ability to listen to and trust your inner voice, too. While Ellie calls the voice your intuition, I call it the Holy Spirit speaking to you. If you desire to fully live out the purpose and destiny for your life, you're going to have to remove the distractions in your life so you can hear clearly what your next divine steps are.

Jeremiah 29:11 says, "For I know the plans I have for you,' declares the LORD, 'plans to prosper you and not to harm you, plans to give you hope and a future.'" If your purpose is unclear to you at this time, don't worry about it. Just keep seeking God and ask Him to speak to you and show you your next steps, and enjoy the journey in the meantime. Greg Anderson says, *"Focus on the journey, not the destination. Joy is found not in finishing an activity, but in doing it."* Your destination is a divine one. Trust it and allow your dreams to reveal the real reasons you are here. You matter. You have a purpose!

⌘ *Reflecting On My Purpose*

I now realize that nothing in my past was a waste of time. Everything that has happened in my life so far was all a part of the plan, even the pain. I want you to know that one of the biggest and most important components of our purpose in life is to glorify, worship, and obey God. We are here to be servants unto the world and to give God the praise for all of our blessings. Trust that God is speaking to you and be open to hearing his voice in all the ways possible. Every step may not be clearly laid out for you, and God may seem silent at times.

Pay attention to the whispers and entertain the messages in your dreams. Be assured that He is speaking to you and working things out for your good. *"And we know that all things work together for good to them that love God, who have been called His purpose."* - Roman 8:28

"Some people say that dreaming gets you nowhere in life. But I say you can't get anywhere in life without dreaming." - **Rose Zadra**

⌘ *Time To Ponder Your Purpose*

Look at your life and the people you've chosen to be a part of your life. Are they destiny seekers or destiny stealers? What's distracting you from your purpose being clearly revealed? How will you choose to remove the distractions in your life so you can live out God's purpose for your life?

_____

_____

_____

_____

_____

_____

_____

_____

_____

_____

CHAPTER 5

Diamonds, Pearls, and Your Purpose

"When we long for life without difficulties, remind us that oaks grow strong in contrary winds and diamonds are made under pressure." – Peter Marshall

We all are diamonds in the eyesight of God, and no diamond is like any other diamond in the world. The way you were shaped and formed can never be duplicated. The mold was broken when God created you. When God said *"For I know the plans I have for you, plans to prosper you and not to harm you, plans to give you hope and a future"* in Jeremiah 29:11, this promise was etched into your DNA.

You are precious, beautiful, one-of-a-kind, and unbreakable. If you inhale this and believe it, what do you have to worry about? If you digest this and let it consume your spirit, you will rediscover exactly why God created you and gave you the purpose and shine that He did. I say rediscover because oftentimes people search for their purpose outside of themselves, but the reason you are here lies within your soul. The beauty of it all is that in your trials, challenges, pain, and obstacles (the pressing), there is a message speaking to you about why you were created, and what you are to do in the world. Your purpose is revealed through the pressures of your life.

Diamonds (crystals of pure carbon) are formed under crushing pressure and intense heat and brought closer to the earth's surface by deep volcanic eruptions. Did you know carbon is the fourth most abundant element in the universe by mass after oxygen, helium, and hydrogen? Did you know that carbon is present in all life forms? Carbon is in fact the one element that is the basis for all life. If diamonds evolve from carbon or crystals of pure carbon, what does that say about you being God's diamond? Furthermore, if diamonds are formed through crushing pressure and intense heat, how can you NOT expect to go through the fire or feel pressed by life's problems? Embracing God's luminosity in your life and showing up and shining like a diamond comes at a cost. Many people talk about and/or desire to be a "diamond," yet they are unwilling to go through the fire or they allow the fire to melt down their magnificence. The truth is, you can't have the shine without the smoldering heat and the painful press.

Did you know God refers to us and sees us as His precious jewels? - In Malachi 3:17, God proclaims *"they shall be Mine,' says the Lord of hosts; on the day that I make them my jewels;"* God has already ordained your value and worth. He's already approved your shine, so you don't need anyone else's permission to twinkle and sparkle like the diamond you are. God entrusted you with amazing power and knows your potential when you can only see the problems you face. You may even perceive yourself and your life to be only "carbon" right now (a diamond in the rough, as they say), but trust and believe you are more than carbon. You are an exquisite creation formed in the image of God with a precious purpose waiting to be revealed. The revealing of your purpose is not only for you. Your purpose was given to you so that you may be a lighthouse for the lost, tired, and weary and to be of great service to the world. If you don't turn on your shine, how will the people who need you see you and get what only you can offer them?

Did you know that when you dim your light, you deny God's craftsmanship and do a disservice to the world? So far, what I've shared in this book has been about the importance of you re-discovering your purpose for your own sake, but please know that your purpose is truly not about you solely. God did not endow you with your gifts, talents, and genius for you to keep it to

PRESSED INTO MY PURPOSE

yourself. You were created to solve a particular problem in the world. Your gifts are to be used to heal and transform the world in some way, and your talents are to be used to ultimately glorify God and lead people into His Kingdom. Everything you've been divinely given was meant to be given away. And when you do all these things through Christ who strengthens you, you will receive the desires of your heart. I want you to rediscover the light within you, your purpose and reason for being here and let it shine, shine, shine! Matthew 5: 14-16 says, *[14] "You are the light of the world. A town built on a hill cannot be hidden. [15] Neither do people light a lamp and put it under a bowl. Instead they put it on its stand, and it gives light to everyone in the house. [16] In the same way, let your light shine before others, that they may see your good deeds and glorify your Father in heaven."*

I mentioned this before, but it's worth repeating. One of the biggest mistakes and "purpose paralyzers" is people comparing their purpose to other people's purpose. God only created one Oprah Winfrey, and no matter how hard someone tries, they will never be her or do what she has been called to do in the world. Your purpose for being in the world may not be one that brings you great fame or fortune. It may not involve you living a life full of glitz and glamour. In fact, it won't look or feel like any other person's purpose. I don't know about you, but I find that to be truly special and remarkable! What a blessing to be chosen, created, and crafted in such a way that you cannot be duplicated. You are irreplaceable, not interchangeable. Doesn't that inspire you to want to wake up your purpose within and walk confidently in the beautiful creation you are? Just the idea of it excites me and reminds me of how special we really are to God and the world. Do not compare your life or your purpose to anyone else's. Theodore Roosevelt says it best, "comparison is the thief of joy." You cannot enjoy your life, your accomplishments, or your success, if you are constantly comparing your experiences to another. You are a diamond. Rare, unique, precious, and beautiful, and it's time to shine. But know there is a price to pay. Life will *press* you into your purpose!

I often talk about diamonds and pearls and use them as metaphors as a way to express the ongoing evolution and transformation I've experienced in my life. Diamonds and pearls are two of the most valuable, precious gems in the world. As you may know, they both evolved from something that appears to be nothing and are transformed into desirable jewels. You may feel like you are nothing or that you are not as great as others, but if you focus on what you see before you, you'll never become the jewel within you.

PRESSED INTO MY PURPOSE

Whomever you admire in your life for their sparkle and shine started out as plain ole carbon just like you and I. The difference is they chose to allow the pressing to polish them into the beautiful diamonds you perceive them to be. You are just like those people. Are you willing and ready to be pressed, shaped, molded, and cut into the diamond that God created you to be?

Your shape and brilliance as a diamond has already been determined. The beauty, sparkle, and radiance you desire (the moment you really shine) won't happen overnight, so be patient with yourself. Over time and with wisdom, your shape and brilliance will emerge just as it is supposed to. Expect the pain of being cut into your brilliance to be a part of the process, however, the pain is increased when you are not in alignment with God's will, plan, and purpose for your life. Quite honestly, even if you *are* in harmony with God's plan, the pressing and cutting is part of the evolution process. It's kind of like this; you can't enjoy the roses without occasionally being pricked by the thorns. Yet, you can reduce the struggle by saying YES to God's purpose, vision, and plan for your life by putting your faith in action and allowing your faith to be bigger than your fears. Don't envy another person's shine because you don't know how much pressing and cutting they endured to become the diamond they are.

Instead, embrace your own unique shape and brilliance.

I thought the following description of various shapes of diamonds was interesting and helps illustrate my point about honoring your own shape and brilliance as a diamond. Read through them and determine which one best fits you at this time in your life or which one you aspire to become. The list, written by Paulina Jewelry, describes the most common diamond shapes and cuts and outlines the character traits of the diamond wearer.

Round Cut: The brilliant round diamond has set the standard for all other diamond shapes and is loved for its sparkle and versatility. In addition to being the most popular and researched shape, a round diamond will typically give you more flexibility in terms of balancing cut, color, and clarity grades while still getting the fire and brilliance you want.

- ◊ **What this says about you**: You are empathic, dependable, and strong, and your first priority is your loved ones.

Oval Cut: This even, perfectly symmetrical stone flatters small hands and short fingers. The diamond's shape gives the illusion of lengthening the hand. When it comes to dazzles, the oval cut definitely has it, thanks to its contrasting silhouette which reflects and retracts light, creating a fiery shine.

- ◊ **What this says about you**: You are very feminine and highly creative. Though you are organized and incredibly disciplined when it comes to getting the job done, after hours, you love to let loose and let your wild side shine through.

Marquise Cut: This elongated shape with pointed ends was inspired by the stunning smile of the Marquise de Pompadour and commissioned by France's Louis XV, who wanted a diamond to mirror his mistress's grin. Today, this diamond is wildly popular. In recent years, it was voted the favorite fancy diamond shape.

- ◊ **What it says about you**: You're sexy, outgoing, impulsive, and zestful with a passion for life's challenges.

Pear Cut: Combining the best of the oval and the marquise cut, its shape is reminiscent of a sparkling tear drop. The unique look of the pear shape helps make it a popular choice for a variety of diamond jewelry. If you choose an elongated pear shape, the length of the diamond creates a subtle slimming effect on the finger.

- ◊ **What it says about you**: You are adventurous and gregarious and love to whoop it up with your wide circle of fabulous funny friends.

Heart Cut: This is perhaps the funkiest shape, embodying sparkle and brilliant beauty. The unique look of the heart-shape diamond helps make it a distinctive choice for a variety of diamond jewelry.

- ◊ **What it says about you**: You are sensitive and romantic and epitomize femininity. Your passionate nature inspires creatively in everyone who surrounds you.

Princess Cut: This square or rectangular cut consists of brilliant cut facets, which produces serious sparkle. It's beautiful brilliance and unique cut makes it a favorite for engagement rings. The princess has pointed corners and is traditionally square in shape.

- ◊ **What it says about you**: If you are drawn to the princess cut, you are an efficient leader who is disciplined and highly organized.

Emerald Cut: What makes this shape different is its pavilion, which is cut with rectangle facets to create a unique optical appearance. Due to its larger, open table, this shape highlights the clarity of a diamond.

◊ **What it says about you**: Women who choose the emerald, asscher, or radiant cut diamonds have a sense of appreciation for the past, and typically hold sentimentality for their heritage and family history.

Asscher Cut: This beautifully unique shape is nearly identical to the emerald cut, except that it is square. Also, this shape's pavilion has rectangular facets in the style of the emerald cut.

◊ **What it says about you**: Women who choose the emerald, Asscher, or radiant cut diamonds have a sense of appreciation for the past, and typically hold sentimentality for their heritage and family history.

Radiant Cut: Trimmed corners are the signature of this diamond, and they help make the radiant cut a popular and versatile choice for jewelry. A radiant cut looks equally beautiful set with either baguette or round sided diamonds. Radiant cut diamonds can vary in their degree of rectangularity.

◊ **What it says about you**: Women who choose the emerald, Asscher, or radiant cut diamonds have a sense of appreciation for the past, and typically hold sentimentality for their heritage and family history.

Cushion Cut: This unique shape has been popular for more than a century. Cushion cut diamonds, also known as "pillow-cut" diamonds, have rounded corners and larger facets to increase their brilliance. These larger facets highlight the diamond's clarity. Cushion cut diamonds are available in shapes ranging from square to rectangular.

- ◊ **What it says about you**: You are one-of-a-kind person, who keeps family tradition and put her family first. Also, your love to pets could be overwhelming.

The diamond cuts depicted in the previous paragraphs while not "scientific," do provide you with an opportunity to realize that your cut, shine, and brilliance is unique to you. God formed you and created you in his image so your shine is inherent. It's up to you whether or not you choose to embrace all your flaws and shine regardless. I cannot stress enough how important it is to NOT compare your purpose and shine to another. Romans 12: 4-8 beautifully expresses my sentiments : *"Just as each of us has one body with many members, and these members do not all have the same function, so in Christ we who are many form one body, and each member belongs to all the others. We have different gifts, according to grace given us. If a man's gift is prophesying, let him use it in proportion to his faith. If it is serving, let him serve; if it is teaching, let him teach; if it is encouraging, let him encourage; if it is contributing to the needs of others, let him give generously; if it is leadership, let him govern diligently; if it is showing mercy, let him do it cheerfully."* Never forget that you are a unique jewel in God's treasure chest!

As the oyster creates a pearl from a grain of sand through irritation, it becomes a precious jewel that the world admires and adores. The world may perceive the grain of sand (you) as small and insignificant, but to the oyster (God), you are a unique and resilient creation. Think about all the grains of sand on the beach or in the ocean. How is it that one grain of sand in particular gets miraculously lodged inside the oyster? From a spiritual perspective, let's call it divine intervention. It was just meant to be, exactly like you were meant to be, and thus you've been placed inside God's masterpiece workshop (the oyster) and with some irritations in life, you become a pearl, a precious jewel.

My dyslexia was an irritant for most of my life. I was challenged, I failed, and many times I felt hopeless because of all the obstacles I had to overcome in my life. Dyslexia was like that small grain of sand that gets lodged in your shoe and you just can't seem to get it out. I questioned God and wondered why He had placed this irritation in my life that caused me to question my intelligence, dishonor my value, and it affected my self-worth for many years. I didn't understand that God was shaping, molding, and cultivating me into an imperfect, yet perfect, pearl for the world to see. Through trials, temptations, tribulations, tests, and disappointments and with God's grace I emerged a pearl. Today, I am grateful for who I've become and for how God has purposely polished my purpose. I no longer question His plan; I trust and know that I've been pressed into the diamond and pearl He envisioned.

What irritants do you have in your life right now? What people, events, or circumstances are not allowing you to take your rightful place in God's master workshop (the oyster)? Don't let your irritants keep you from evolving into the precious gem that you are. God never promised that living your purpose would be easy, but you'll one day look in the mirror and see your true radiance and brilliance. You'll be able to say, "Through it all, I prevailed." When you approach the gates of heaven, God will say, "Job well done, good and faithful servant."

Before you begin to ponder your purpose, reflect again on what I shared earlier in the chapter. When God said, *"For I know the plans I have for you, plans to prosper you and not to harm you, plans to give you hope and a future"* (Jeremiah 29:11). The promise was made, and God always delivers His promise. He could have chosen anyone to carry out a part of His global plan, but He chose you. He already knows what you will endure to complete the divine assignment, which is why He equipped you with all you need to emerge resilient even in the midst of trouble, challenges, irritants, and pressure. He's provided the provision, and if you have full, total, and complete faith in His plan, you will become the diamond or pearl you were created to be.

⌘ *Reflecting On My Purpose*

Sometimes in my past life, I felt like God had singled me out and had given me more pressure than what I thought I could handle. I wanted to give up and quit more times than I can count. There were so many times when I asked, "Why me, God?" While intuitively I knew that God was working His magic in my life, it did not make the pain and pressure easier to deal with. Yet, somehow I found the courage within to trust His word, vision, and plan for my life. I found the strength to endure the pressing irritation. And while I still feel the press every so often, I have evolved into a precious gem, a jewel that has a shine like no other. I am God's diamond!

> *"Diamonds were nothing more than carbon, but carbon in a crystal lattice that made it the hardest known mineral in nature. That was the way we all were headed. I was sure of it. We were destined to be diamond."* - **Alan Bradley**

⌘ *Time To Ponder Your Purpose*

Take some time to think about all the irritants that you've experienced in your life (or are experiencing now). What are they shaping you into? What are you being prepared for? What qualities and character traits are you developing as a result of the irritation? What is the purpose for your press? Start connecting the dots to your divine purpose!

_____
_____
_____
_____
_____
_____
_____
_____
_____

CHAPTER 6

Free Will vs. God's Will

"I don't mean to say that I have already achieved these things or that I have already reached perfection. But I press on to possess that perfection for which Christ Jesus first possessed me." - Philippians 3:12

Our divine destiny is already determined. Although God has a perfect purpose for our lives and has already created the vision, He also gave us the power of free will. The way I see it, we have two choices: to be in alignment with God's will and carry out *His* plan or exercise our own free will and create an alternate destiny. God's roadmap for our destination isn't always crystal clear to the human eye, and it can be hard sometimes to hear His voice and directions. Because of this, we start charting our own course based on *our* needs, wants, desires, and even fears. This is often when we get in trouble, get sidetracked, lose focus, or end up traveling dangerous roads and taking unnecessary detours.

PRESSED INTO MY PURPOSE

It is only when we summon God's voice as a constant compass and follow His lead that we arrive at our divine destination and fulfill God's purpose for our lives.

By the time I graduated from high school, I knew I was unstoppable, so I decide to work toward achieving the highest educational degree that I possibly could. I wrote down a list of goals, as well as potential obstacles for each goal, side by side and then I found scriptures in the Bible related to keeping the faith and overcoming challenges. This was more than just a writing exercise; it was a contract between God and I. I knew that if I put my faith in God, listened to His direction, and put my plan into action, I could accomplish all the goals on my list. I placed the list inside of my Bible and there it stayed. Over the next years, I frequently reflected and meditated on my list and began to put my faith in action. Every time I referred to my list, I prayed that God would remove any obstacles that might arise on my journey to fulfill my purpose.

I was very clear and intentional about my prayers. I specifically asked God to open doors of opportunity and to provide the financial resources I needed to invest in my college education. I didn't sit around waiting for God to act; instead I trust my intuition and began applying for student loans, grants, and other forms of financial aid. I was so determined to become a college student that I even asked my family for monetary donations. I must admit, I was a bit reluctant to ask my family for help, but I put my fears and shame to the side and asked anyway.

One day, years later, while talking on the phone to my daughter, Catina, who was in the military, I shared with her my dream of getting my bachelor's degree. I shared my concerns about how I was going to have to come up with the money for my tuition. I didn't directly ask her for any money, I was simply making conversation. Although I had many thoughts and some concerns about getting the money, deep inside, I knew God was going to provide for me. I had to believe in His promise because, after all, He had never failed me in the past. A few days later, I went to the mailbox and there was a letter from my daughter. To my surprise, enclosed was a check for the full amount of my tuition. I was ecstatic! I felt so overwhelmed with gratitude and excitement that I could have burst wide open. I immediately called my daughter and thanked her for contributing to my education. My dream was about to come true. What a blessing! You never know who might bless you with their generosity. All you have to do is believe, have faith, and trust God. And put your pride to the side, I must add.

PRESSED INTO MY PURPOSE

Despite having dyslexia, I enrolled in the community college in my hometown. I could only afford to take one class per semester and raise a family. Times and circumstances were much different for women in the 1970s and opportunities for well-paying jobs weren't very fruitful. No matter what, I was determined to earn my degree. My first class was an art appreciation course which spawned my love for the arts. I couldn't believe it; I was actually a college student! I had such a feeling of accomplishment, and it was only my first class. I felt so inspired each time I went to class and loved the enthusiasm my instructor had. She knew how to bring the material to life with her passion or the arts, and the class was so interesting and thought provoking that I soon became engulfed in her passion and became passionate too. I vividly remember chatting with her during one of our class breaks. She shared bits and pieces of her amazing journey of discovering the arts, and then she began to talk about her own story of having dyslexia and how she had to overcome many obstacles in her life. You have no idea how hearing her story blessed my soul. I needed to hear that story, and I believe God put this woman on my path to encourage me to keep going forward despite my dyslexia. After hearing her story, I felt renewed, determined, and was energized with great gusto to keep moving forward, full steam ahead to fulfill my purpose in life.

Flash forward after many classes, challenges, setbacks, and accomplishments to my graduate studies of South-Side Community College where I was earning my associate's degree in Human Services. I couldn't believe I had earned my first degree. I was so elated and at the same time afraid to stop there, for fear I wouldn't return to school. I decided to transfer my community college credits to St. Paul's College, a four-year degree program, which was about a twenty-minute drive from my home. The next two years were exciting, testing, overwhelming, and so fulfilling at the same time. It was sometimes hectic to balance raising a family and being a college student, but I was determined to achieve my goals. Sure, there were many times I wanted to quit and give up, but I knew this was a part of my destiny and that obtaining my degrees would allow me to better provide for my family.

My dyslexia certainly created some obstacles for me along the way, however, I was relentless in pursuing my goals. I had to ask for help, work at my own pace, stay up late, and do whatever it took to complete my assignments and get good grades. During the four years as a college student, I felt the press, the stress, the heat, the cutting, and weight of wanting to become more than I was before I started. It was not easy by far, but I was willing to be pressed so that I could eventually come out a polished diamond. I eventually graduated from St. Paul's College with a bachelor's in Organizational Management. I went back to my Bible to assess where I was with my goals and felt so much pride as I checked off several of the goals I had listed. God had surely delivered on His promises. Despite everything I experienced over the past four years, I made it through with the grace of God. I was so thankful, and knew there was more for me to experience, so I was still feeling unstoppable!

While reflecting on my goals, I began to envision my ultimate life. God was clearly nudging me to continue dreaming, to fully actualize my purpose, go for more, and to trust in Him along the way. I added a few more goals to the list, and one of them was to obtain my master's and doctoral degree. Unfortunately, I had no idea what I wanted to major in. My seemingly smooth educational journey took an interesting turn over the next few years. I was still feeling pretty unstoppable, and I believed I could do almost anything. I was ready to return to the classroom and earn my degrees.

At first, I thought I wanted to become a school counselor, so I enrolled into Virginia State College to begin the process. After my first class, I realized that was not what I really wanted to do. It just didn't feel right, and I wasn't as inspired as I had previously been.

After finishing my first class, I dropped out. I had always been fascinated by many of my previous teachers and admired how they were able to captivate their students and teach with so much passion and excitement. So I thought I would become a teacher as well. Soon after leaving Virginia State College, I enrolled into Old Dominion College to become an adult education teacher. After completing two classes, I realized that was not right for me either and dropped out to take a break. I really needed to get clear on what I wanted. Besides, I felt like I was wasting time and money.

While I believed achieving my academic goals was a part of my purpose and essential to God's vision and plan for my life, I soon realized I was allowing "free will" to get in the way of God's way. During the time between receiving my bachelor's and finishing my master's, I had not been listening closely to God's voice. Instead, I was doing what I thought I should do based on outer circumstances instead of the compass within. I kind of got caught up in chasing what appeared to be the right thing to do instead of allowing God to order my next steps. Rather than acting on my own free will any further, I decided to ask for and wait on God's next command for the journey.

PRESSED INTO MY PURPOSE

While working as the Senior Center Director, I was transferred for a short time to the central office to serve as the Nutrition Specialist. Surprisingly, after being there for a while, they offered to pay for some classes to help me become more knowledgeable in my position. It was a requirement that I enroll into Virginia State College to begin my studies in nutrition, so I did. It's amazing how God works! I loved my position as the Senior Center Director and had not imagined leaving it until I retired, actually. God made a move and not only put me into a position that I had not considered, but an educational path I hadn't considered, either. Prior to this master move, I was struggling to determine what my next educational step would be, and then God stepped in with ease and grace and opened up an unexpected door. Although I had no prior interest in nutrition, I knew instinctively this was the "right" next step, so I put my own free will to the side and said, "Yes Lord, I will be obedient to your command."

Once again, I enrolled in Virginia State College and began taking classes. I got off to a great start and was making excellent grades. I enjoyed my classes and felt like I was on track an on the right path at the right time. My final two classes were Chemistry courses and were all I needed to complete my degree, but I struggled. For the life of me, I couldn't seem to pass these final courses. I hired tutors, but to no avail. I felt so defeated and devastated. I couldn't believe I had come this far, but could not finish. I began to question my purpose and (truthfully) God, a little bit. I thought to myself, "God, you said this was the right path for me. I know you didn't bring me this far to leave me." I was frustrated and didn't know what to do. If I couldn't pass the classes with a tutor, I believed there was no way possible for me to finish my degree, so once again, I dropped out. There was a glimmer of hope during this dark time, however. I had taken enough classes to maintain my position as Nutrition Specialist, so at least I still had money coming in to support my family. I went back to focusing on my job, but the sting of incompletion continued to consume me as the days went by.

In 1998, I became the assistant pastor of my local church, which was such a fulfilling role for me. I thoroughly enjoyed the opportunity to be of service and use my spiritual gifts in the church; after all, they are God's gifts. I joyfully served in this capacity for about nine years, then, in 2007, I became the lead pastor. In the midst of trying to raise a family and pursue my education, I had to answer the one of the biggest calls of my life: to lead and minister to the people of my church. I was juggling a lot of things in my life and, although there were times I grew weary and wanted to give up, I kept pressing forward. After taking some time off from school, I was about to reach a point of giving up on completing my master's degree. Besides, my plate was full and I was having extreme feelings of doubt about ever finishing.

Just when I decided I was going to give up, I ran across an advertisement about a biblical institution in my area called Berean Light Institute. I had never heard anything about this school, but it sounded interesting. Why not pursue a Christian educational path this time, since I was already functioning in a pastoral capacity within my church? I was moving toward the end of my work-life career and was ready to say yes to God's next assignment. I was also being positioned to take on the lead role as head pastor of my church and this advertisement seemed to be pointing me into a new direction. Maybe God didn't want me to finish that degree in nutrition. Maybe He wanted me to move away from the secular education and obtain a Christian-based education. I waited, and then I waited a little while longer to hear God speak and command my next steps.

During my wait, a scripture rose up in my spirit. II Timothy 2:15 says, "Study to show thyself approved unto God, a workman that needing not to be ashamed, rightly dividing the word of truth." This scripture deeply resonated with me at this particular time. My church members had grown comfortable with me in the assistant pastor's role, but I wondered how they would receive me as head pastor. I believe God put this scripture in my spirit to let me know that my next step was to obtain a degree that would prepare me to lead His church. That was it. That was the sign I was waiting for. And yet again, that following fall, I enrolled in class—this time at Berean Light Institute, where I eventually earned my bachelor's degree in Biblical Studies. Two years later, I began working on my master's degree in Biblical Studies and completed that degree as well. I was feeling great and still being pulled towards completing my doctorate. Unfortunately, the Berean Light Institute did not offer any doctoral programs.

I searched and searched to find the right doctoral program and eventually discovered the Andersonville Theological Seminary School located in Camilla, Georgia. I applied to the program, was accepted, and began pursuing my doctoral degree in Biblical Counseling. I couldn't believe it! The dream I had as young girl was finally becoming a reality. Once again, there were very challenging moments during my studies. My dyslexia seemed to get in the way many times. I struggled in some classes and did very well in others. I had come so far and had been through so much that I refused to quit or drop out. I was determined to finish, no matter what. I knew that my journey was not in vain and that I had to encounter the tests, trials, tribulations, storms, and pain for a reason. They were all a part of God's big plan for my life. I turned to God and my Bible very heavily while working on finishing this degree.

One scripture in particular helped me make it through. Philippians 4: 13 reminded me that:

"I can do all things through Christ which strengtheneth me." I knew that it was going to take a supernatural intervention for me to complete my degree.

The words of the Apostle Paul also helped me keep pressing for the prize. *"Brethren, I count not myself to have apprehended: but this one thing I do, forgetting those things which are behind, and reaching forth unto those things which are before, I press toward the mark for the prize of the high calling of God in Christ Jesus."*(Philippians 3:13). Through my whole educational journey, I knew there was a higher purpose for my life. There was more for me to discover, learn and do. Most importantly, there was more for me to become. Just because I finished my degree didn't mean that God was through cutting, shaping, and molding me for my divine assignment in the world. The pressing was not over. The evolution of your purpose does not stop once you discover it. Your purpose only ends when you take your last breath.

You'll notice I have not directly stated what I believe my purpose is at this point. In many ways, I was pretty sure of my higher calling, yet I was still searching for the ultimate purpose. Sometimes I allowed my free will to guide my path, and other times I believed in and followed God's *will* for my life. It was during the times I exercised my own free will that I struggled the most, lacking clarity, faith and guidance. But when I fully trusted God, waited on His direction and followed His lead, the struggle was decreased. I say decreased because there's a misconception that there will be *no* trouble, obstacles, or challenges when we follow God. That is not necessarily true. God reminds us of this scripture in Philippians 1: 6, as we follow his lead. *"Being confident of this very thing, that he which hath begun a good work in you will perform it until the day of Jesus Christ."* My translation is if we trust and have confidence in the purpose that God has put inside of us, He will finish and reveal that purpose to us until the end of days when we see Jesus. Discovering and living your purpose won't always be crystal clear to the eye, but it will always be clear in your heart. Read God's word, meditate on it, and summon His voice and commands in all your endeavors. This will keep you in God's will!

PRESSED INTO MY PURPOSE

So how do you discover what your *real* purpose is in life? You're going to hear a lot of variations about how to find out what your purpose is. Some of those strategies will work for you and others may not. Just remember that you are unique and what might work for someone else may not be right for you. The most important thing to remember is that YOU have a purpose. Keep asking God what your purpose is and ask Him to reveal it in a way that your heart can't deny.

Here are a few questions that may help you become one step closer to revealing your purpose. Take some time and write down your responses to see if you can find a common thread that leads you to your ultimate purpose.

- What do I get excited about that I could do all day and get lost in it?

- What would I do all day without getting paid for it?

- What worldly issue gets me fired up to the point I feel like I must do something about it?

- What do I have an extreme passion for?

- What motivates me to do better and make a difference in the world?

- What pulls me into action?

- What natural talents and skills do I have that people often seek out?

- What is my heart telling me to do?

Regardless of what your answers are, you have been created and called to serve the world in some way that ultimately leads God's people back to Him and the kingdom. God will reveal your purpose in so many different ways. That's why it's critical that you stay in alignment with God's word. It's essential that you invite Him in daily to order your steps and guide you on your journey. Your destiny has already been determined. The vision has been created. The purpose is in place. God is waiting for you to say yes and co-create the plan to carry out His divine assignment for your life. Stay in harmony with *God's* will for your life and your purpose *will* be revealed to you.

⌘ *Reflecting On My Purpose*

> It seemed like I was never going to complete my educational goals, but, if you recall, when I wrote those goals in my Bible, I declared that I would be unstoppable. Not only did I believe in my ability to overcome and persevere, but I knew that if I put my faith in action, I could do all things through God who strengthens me. During this educational marathon, I realized the power of embracing God's will for my life instead of creating struggle by exercising my own free will. How can you become unstoppable in your pursuit of your purpose? How will you trust more in God's will than your own free will?

"Trust in the LORD with all thine heart;
and lean not unto thine own understanding. In all thy
ways acknowledge him, and he shall direct thy paths."
- *Proverbs 3:5-6*

⌘ *Time To Ponder Your Purpose*

I found this exercise on the Steve Pavlina blog, and he shares insight on how to discover your true (real purpose). Take out a blank sheet of paper and write the following at the top of the page. "What is my true purpose?" Next write any and all thoughts and feelings that come to you. Don't over think it. Just let the ideas and thoughts flow on paper. Repeat the steps until what you write makes you cry. Steve says this is how you discover your true purpose.

_____

_____

_____

_____

_____

_____

_____

_____

_____

⌘ *Time To Ponder Your Purpose (Part 2)*

Reflect back on your life and determine all the ways you've exercised your free will vs. following God's will and see if you can see what difference it made.

CHAPTER 7

My Higher Calling

"The first time I walked on a stage, I knew that was what I was created to do. I knew that there was a calling and a sense of purpose in my life that gave me fulfillment and a sense of destiny." – Bishop TD Jakes

My spiritual journey consciously began at about the age twenty. It was at this time I truly introduced Jesus Christ as my personal savior. For the first time, I intentionally began building a personal relationship with God instead of following a religion. I was taught to religiously attend church on Sunday, read my Bible, and pray, and while doing those things helped me establish and maintain my faith, I knew there was something more to be gained.

Religion taught me about many things or acts that I "should" do in order to have a relationship with God, yet it all felt so external. I think I had the belief that although God loved me and cared for me, He was somewhat outside of me. I also had the deep belief that

PRESSED INTO MY PURPOSE

God wanted more for me and I could receive more from Him if I had a personal relationship with Him.

I grew up in the church. I was always attending church with my sister or one of the community mothers. When I moved to Washington, DC, I found a church I wanted to attend. I made it a point to try and attend church every Sunday and when I didn't, things just didn't feel right. I actually felt guilty sometimes and thought I was letting God down. I would soon discover that God's expectations surpassed the religious expectations of attending church, praying and reading my Bible. It became evident that I must do more than attend church on Sunday then do whatever I wanted on the other days of the week. God was certainly loving, guiding, and protecting me the other six days of the week, and it was time for me to honor Him seven days a week.

While still living in Washington, DC, I had a very vivid dream. I remember lying in a hospital bed. I thought I was asleep. I was in total darkness. I wondered if I had died or thought maybe I was having some sort of out of body experience. Yet, I recall hearing my conscious or subconscious—I'm not really sure which one—speaking to me. At the same time, I saw my life pass before my eyes. I saw everything I had done in life, big and small. I saw every lie I told, every sneaky and deceitful thing I had done. In the dream, I remember crying out for God's forgiveness and repenting. I was dressed in a long white dress and white slippers.

Suddenly, I felt the presence of someone else in the room. Maybe it was a nurse or someone else. I wasn't sure, but I knew I was not alone. I instinctively knew this presence was a female. I then heard her voice distinctively whispering the Lord's Prayer in my ear. She told me to repeat the prayer over and over, and I did. To my amazement, when I lifted my head up, I saw two hands reaching down for me. At first I felt cold, but when I saw that the two hands were draped in long white sleeves, I saw a bright white light. The light began to make me feel warm, and I was overcome with an overwhelming sense of peace and joy. Suddenly I woke up. Even today, I don't know for sure if this was a dream, a vision, or something I experienced for real. It felt real, and when I think about it, it still feels like it actually happened.

After this experience, I knew I needed and wanted to do more. I knew I needed to develop a personal relationship with God, one that extended far beyond the expectations of religious acts. I felt a sense of urgency to find a church home and start building a truly intimate relationship with God. When I moved back to my hometown in Virginia, I was on a mission to find a church where I could be of great service to my community. I started attending various churches in search of my church home. I asked God to lead me to the church where He wanted me to be so I could serve how He wanted me to serve. Shortly after my request, a neighbor came to my house and began witnessing about God's salvation for us as Christians. I was open to receiving her message and listened with an open heart. After she left, I sat down on the steps in the back of my house and read the Sinner's Prayer from a pamphlet she had given me. For the first time, this prayer spoke to my spirit in ways it had never done before. I felt the same warmth, peace, radiance, and joy that I did in the dream I shared earlier.

I truly believed this was a sign, the answer to my request for help in finding my new church home. I knew God was guiding me to this place where I could develop an intimate relationship with Him and be of service. I decided to be obedient and attend my neighbor's church. All it took was one visit, and I was sure I was in the right place. I knew this was where God wanted me to be. Honestly, it was kind of a "love at first sight" moment, and I had a twenty-year love affair with this church. I began to learn Biblical principles that helped me understand the difference between religion and relationship with God and the difference between being saved and having salvation.

Being saved means you have been born again and have accepted Jesus Christ as your savior, whereas salvation means you live everyday like you were born again. Salvation requires you to seek God daily, pray, meditate, and practice forgiveness and repentance ongoing until you take your last breath. Before I decided to build an intimate relationship with God, I was a saved Christian going to church. Today, I seek my salvation with every breath I take.

I served in many capacities during those twenty years. I was a Sunday School Teacher, a Missionary, and sang in the choir. My children (Antonio and Catina) and I grew up together in this church.-Proverbs 22:6 says, *"Train up a child in the way he should go: and when he is old, he will not depart from it."* I wanted to teach my children how to have a relationship with God beyond attending church on Sundays. This was one of the best gifts I believe I could have given them. We had countless spiritual and transformational moments in this church, but after twenty years of service, God called me to another vineyard to do work for His kingdom.

My next spiritual assignment was one I was not expecting, seeking, or desiring to tell the truth, yet God had a different plan and purpose for my life. Many people clamor at the chance to become the leader of sheep, a pastor of a church, but I truly didn't want any part of that position. The thought of taking on such a prestigious role scared me to death. I worried whether I was able to live up to God's expectations and handle such a big responsibility. I was especially frightened when God spoke to me saying, "The blood of the people is on my head." Can you imagine what it feels like to have God Almighty speak those words to you? I was not feeling very confident about caring for the souls of God's people and worried about the sacrifice if would require. I was reluctant to say yes, but was reminded of the scripture John 3:16, "For God so loved the world that He gave his only begotten Son, that whosoever believeth in him should not perish, but have everlasting life." God made the ultimate sacrifice for me and there was no way I was going to say no to His command. The sacrifices I would be required to make as a pastor would never compare to God's sacrifice.

I wasn't sure how I would manage this great expectation, but I was reminded of what Jesus told His disciples. They were empowered with His declaration that they had been given all authority in heaven and on earth, therefore they were to go and make disciples of all the nations, baptizing them in the name of the Father and the son and the Holy Spirit. Jesus instructed them to teach these new disciples to obey all commands He had given them and to be sure that He was with them always, even to the end of the age. It was my time to stand in this position of power with patience, poise, presence, and the prevailing leadership of God. This assignment, by far, was the biggest and most sacred act in my purpose journey, and with knees knocking, I said yes once again to be pressed into my purpose.

Was I really prepared for this next assignment? In many ways I believed I was, but there was quite a bit of uncertainty in my spirit. Do you feel like God is calling you into your higher purpose? Do you feel like there is something bigger and possibly even scary that you are being drawn towards? Are you resisting your greatest purpose because you feel like it will be too hard, that you might fail, or that you are not equipped to fulfill the purpose? Don't let the fear and anxiety you feel about your calling keep you from the blessing hidden in the potential pain and discomfort. There are great dividends you will reap when you say yes to your higher call, even when it seems impossible. If you are desiring a life and a lifestyle where your needs are exceeded, a life that fulfills you and pleases God, and a life where you find great pleasure and joy doing what God created you to do, you must obey the commands of God as it relates to your purpose.

PRESSED INTO MY PURPOSE

Isaiah 1:19 says, *"If you are willing and obedient, you shall eat the good of the land."* Many people want the milk and honey, but do not want to obey God's commands. When you truly trust God, you will say yes to your higher calling even if you are afraid. There may be a trembling in your voice, but say yes. Your knees may be shaking, but say yes. You may not be able to see the end, but say yes. You may not feel fully equipped, but say yes anyway. God already knows your fear and concerns, but He's calling you into your higher purpose. He would not call you into something He did not think you could handle and succeed at. Instead of worrying about all the reasons it won't work or how afraid you are, conjure up all the reasons it will work and how successful you'll be at stepping into your purpose. I can assure you that your highest calling will be the scariest. If it were an easy task, everyone would be doing it. If you want to become a brilliant diamond that shines in the world, you've got to be willing to endure the pressing heat that will create your sparkling transformation.

You only live once! Every moment is an opportunity to live fully and fulfilled. How long you live does not compare to *how* you live. What will you do with the gifts, talents, opportunities, and resources that have been made available to you? It's God who gives you the gifts, talents, and resources and places the opportunities before you. How will you give back to the giver? Your ability to sing, write, compose, dance, create, heal, or inspire are all gifts from God. He gave you those gifts to use in the world to be of service in your higher calling. You may be thinking *"why me or are you sure God,"* but be certain that your awesome, all powerful creator did not make a mistake in choosing you for your higher calling. I challenge you to search your heart today, summon the voice of God and allow His voice to tell you what your higher calling is. It may come as a whisper, a thundering clap or show up in an unexpected way, but be on the lookout and be open to not only hearing the call, but be sure to answer it with an unwavering YES!

It's easy to think God made a mistake in crafting such a big purpose for you. Don't you dare for one second believe that. There is no such thing as a mistake in God's world. He created you and knew you before you were born. He's placed inside of you everything you need to carry out your purpose in life. God wants you to succeed. He wants you to be at peace, to be happy, and to live a fulfilled life. He also wants you to glorify Him in everything you do. God has also called you to go make disciples of all the nations and to do it by operating in your purpose. God is not concerned with your challenges, your pain, or the obstacles you may be facing. He's not concerned with your lack of education, finances, or family support. God doesn't care what kind of house you live in or what city you live in. All the circumstances you see before you that tell you it's impossible to live in and on purpose mean nothing to God. He can remove all your doubts, worries, fears, and challenges in the blink of an eye. In fact, when you say yes to your higher calling, He will begin to create a miraculous change in your life in such a way that it will become unrecognizable. Don't let anything, anyone or any circumstance keep you from saying yes to your higher calling, even if you are not yet sure of what it is.

Believe you have a purpose. Believe that you were created perfectly imperfect. Believe you are great and there is greatness within you. Believe that God can and will do all things when you believe in Him and His supernatural power. I believe God created me to be just who I am today. He designed me to be a one-of-a-kind masterpiece just like you. Having dyslexia was not some fluke stroke of bad luck. I believe God gave that to me, too. I once used it as a crutch and saw it as a disability, but today I believe it is a gift. Dyslexia has allowed me to be more patient and compassionate in my life. It caused me to have greater faith, to persevere, and to deny the defeat it can bring. I became more observant and intuitive as a result of having dyslexia. Dyslexia is considered to be a disability, but I refuse to allow it to disable me. Dyslexia gave me an internal drive to be more, do more, and have more in my life. Instead of allowing it to become a stumbling block, I courageously chose to use it as stepping stones toward fulfilling my higher calling in life, my true divine purpose.

My ultimate purpose in life was not to travel the world, to live in the bright lights and big city, to become a schoolteacher, or to even obtain higher education. I know and believe that my higher calling was to pastor and lead God's people. That is *my purpose* in the world. Look at the journey God took me on so that I could arrive at *this* place. I never imagined that my journey would lead me to be the pastor of my church in my hometown. When I left Virginia and headed to Washington, DC, I just knew my purpose would be found away from home. Isn't God amazing? When you set out to discover your purpose and begin the journey of finding your higher calling, there is no telling what you will encounter or experience on your path. The most important piece of advice I can share with you is to *believe* God is leading you in the right direction. It's so necessary for you to ask for His guidance along the way and to listen for your next steps. When you receive direction, say yes and put your faith into action. Move your feet, even when you are unsure of where you are heading. Dr. Martin Luther King Jr. said it best, "*Faith is taking the first step even when you don't see the whole staircase."*

Have faith in yourself, your gifts, your talents, and your abilities. God did not make a mistake in creating you just the way you are. This act alone will empower you to confidently carry out the higher calling on your life. Over the years, I've learned to love me, the true authentic person I am today. I am free from within and liberated from the world. I accept myself for who I am—God's diamond! I am prepared as a result of the pressing to fully carry out my purpose in life. I've learned to be honest and truthful and make no attempts to fool others. I've learned to be a person of integrity by acting the same with others as I would alone. I've learned how to live the golden rule and treat others how I want to be treated. I've learned to forgive so that I too will be forgiven. Nothing was luck. Nothing was a mistake. It all was a part of God's big plan for me. Every step I took was leading me to my higher calling to pastor a church and lead God's people back to His kingdom.

NOW is the time for you to seek, answer, and respond to *your* higher calling. If you really want to discover and experience it, you must be daring, diligent, and determined to be all that God created you to be. Take a bold step today and BELIEVE you have a great purpose. Be unwavering today and commit to answering your higher call. Be obedient and surrender your plans and your will over to God. Be brave and take faithful steps even if you are afraid. Be not moved or paralyzed by your circumstances, instead command those mountains to move out of our way.

Stop being religious and start developing an intimate relationship with God. Don't worry about having it all together, just get on the same page with God and say YES to your higher calling, no matter what. *God's got it and He's got you, too!* The phone is ringing. It's God. Will you pick up the phone?

⌘ *Reflecting On My Purpose*

> When I committed to developing a personal and intimate relationship with God, I had no idea what kind of impact it would have on my life. Deep down inside, I knew it must be done. I'm so thankful that I know Jesus and God personally and that I have transitioned from being saved to seeking my salvation one day at a time. Having a personal relationship with God helped me discover, embrace, and operate in my higher calling, and I am blessed to experience God's vision for my life.

"There is no chance, no destiny, no fate that can circumvent or hinder or control the firm resolve of a determine soul." - **Ellen Wheeler Wilcox**

⌘ *Time to Ponder Your Purpose*

Do you have a personal relationship with God or are you a religious Christian? Are you saved or are you seeking your salvation? What will you do today to develop or strengthen your personal relationship with God? How can you make it more intimate so you can say yes to your higher calling?

CHAPTER 8

Answering Your Call and Serving with Purpose

"If you want to know the past, to know what has caused you, look at yourself in the present, for that is the past's effect. If you want to know your future, then look at yourself in the present, for that is the cause of the future." - Majjhima Nikaya

Have you received God's call for your life? Has He informed you of your divine assignment for your life? Maybe you are finding it difficult to clearly know when God has "called" you to complete a specific assignment in your life. In some ways "the call" can be hard to explain, but I assure you, when God calls you to carry out a mission, your soul will *know* that it is God speaking to you. His message to each of us is the same, however, His tone is universal. Trust and believe that when God speaks to you, you'll know because His voice calms, comforts, convicts, encourages, enlightens, leads, reassures, and stills you. When you are feeling confused about the messages and voices you hear, just remember, God says, "be still and know that I am God" (Psalms 46:10).

From a devastated, insecure little second grader to being called to shepherd a flock of God's people has been the most pivotal moment in my life. My life's journey was preparing me for "my calling" all along. Every setback was a setup for what God had in store for me. Every pain I endured prepared me to be patient, and kind and to show compassion for the people I would encounter in the future. Every challenge I faced equipped me with the insight, wisdom, and discernment I'd need to help other people overcome their challenges. I now understand that life was not happening *to* me, but rather life was happening *for* me. God took me through many challenges to prepare me for the ultimate calling on my life.

I was called into the role of assistant pastor of the New Life Christian Center in Emporia, Virginia in 1998 and then head pastor in 2007. The premise of my church is to help people who are lost in the world find their way back to the fold of God. We are known as the "hospital beside the road" where the lonely, bruised, scorned, and hurt come for rest, peace, hope, healing, and restoration. We truly allow people to come as they are at New Life Christian Center. Often times, those who are recently released from prison find their way to us. We have impacted and helped transform the lives of countless men and women who come through our doors. I was called to introduce and re-introduce the lost to Christ and teach them how to develop a relationship with God.

All of my education, experiences, challenges, and defeats have prepared me for this one moment in time. It all makes sense now, and I am grateful that God created this vision and plan for my life. We are all given gifts that are to be given back to the world through service. What an amazing opportunity it is to be able to use all of myself in service to others. That's what we are here to do. That's what you are here to do. Serving as the head pastor of my church is the most fulfilling work I've ever had. In addition to ministering to the congregation's spiritual needs, we also assist our members with job searches, financial support, a food pantry, and other programs to help them with their basic needs. We work with local organizations to support the members of our church and community, and we offer a variety of programs for children, the elderly, the sick, and the incarcerated, as well. I have a wonderful team of people, including my sister, Pricilla, who helps us be of great service to those with the greatest need. We are using our spiritual gifts to serve the world!

Do you know what your spiritual gifts are? I'm not talking about your areas of expertise or even the things you may be passionate about. I'm referring to the natural, God-given talents you have that you easily and effortlessly do. Your spiritual gifts are supernatural abilities given to you by the Holy Spirit that endow you to glorify Jesus and exalt His name in your service or ministry to the world. God has given you many abilities, but spiritual gifts in particular can be traced back to the Bible. I mention this because it's important to know the difference between a skill and a spiritual gift. You may be skilled at drawing, but that may not necessarily be a spiritual gift. You may be a talented singer, but only when you use your voice to exhort God is it considered a spiritual gift, and we are to use our spiritual gifts to lead people to Christ and build up His church until He returns.

I highly encourage you to learn more and do your own research on spiritual gifts. In Romans 12, 1 Corinthians, and Ephesians chapter 4 you will learn more about spiritual gifts. When you accept Christ as your personal savior (becoming saved), you are endowed with at least one spiritual gift, yet it's possible to have more than one. Get out your Bible today and start learning more about spiritual gifts. You can start by reading the following passages:

- Ephesians 4:7
- I Corinthians 12:7-11
- I Corinthians 7:7
- I Peter 4:10

Here, you will discover what kind of gifts you have. Spiritual gifts are to be used in love through service to others. Read the following scriptures to learn more about using your spiritual gifts as an act of love:

- Romans 11:36
- Colossians 1:16
- Revelation 4:11
- Ephesians 4:11-13
- 1 Corinthians 1:7
- 1 Peter 4:10
- John 16:13-14
- John 15:8

When you give your life to God, you are given supernatural abilities (gifts) to solely live out your purpose, glorify Jesus Christ, and help bring people into God's fold (His church). The main difference between natural talents or skills and spiritual gifts is that *only* Christians are given spiritual gifts. Have you personally invited God into your life? Have you been saved and born again? If not, in order to fully activate your spiritual gifts, you must ask God to come into your life and for Jesus to be your personal savior. The only way *to* God is *through* His son Jesus.

Jesus said to him, "I am the way, and the truth, and the life. No one comes to the Father except through me." John 14:6

Becoming saved is a big decision, and I encourage you to seek spiritual counsel from a trusted Christian leader to help you understand what being saved means. I also caution you to not become saved just to discover and utilize your spiritual gifts, but to become saved because you deeply desire to be delivered from your sins and want to live a Godly life. Romans 10:13 says, *"For everyone who calls on the name of the Lord shall be saved."* Essentially, this means that when you ask God to come into your life and believe that Jesus Christ died on the cross for your sins, you will be saved.

1 Peter 3:18-22 says, *"For Christ also suffered once for sins, the righteous for the unrighteous, that he might bring us to God, being put to death in the flesh but made alive in the spirit, in which he went and proclaimed to the spirits in prison, because they formerly did not obey, when God's patience waited in the days of Noah, while the ark was being prepared, in which a few, that is, eight persons, were brought safely through water. Baptism, which corresponds to this, now saves you, not as a removal of dirt from the body but as an appeal to God for a good conscience, through the resurrection of Jesus Christ, who has gone into heaven and is at the right hand of God, with angels, authorities, and powers having been subjected to him."* Once you become saved, the Holy Spirit will activate your spiritual gifts. If you'd like to learn more about how to identify your spiritual gifts, Jeff Carver does an excellent job at explaining what spiritual gifts are and offers you a test to help you determine your own. Check out Jeff's website for more information at spiritualgiftstest.com

God empowers us with spiritual gifts so we can lead, guide, and direct people towards a goal or destination. While this list may not be exhaustive, it will give you an idea of the spiritual gifts outlined in the Bible. Again, these can be found in Romans 12:6-8, 1 Corinthians 12:8-10, 28-30, and Ephesians 4:11.

Administration	Mercy	Faith
Apostleship	Miracles	Giving
Discernment	Pastor/Shepherd	Healing
Knowledge	Serve/Minister	Exhortation
Leadership	Teach	Wisdom
Interpretation of Tongues	Prophecy	Speak in Tongues
Evangelism		

While I won't expand upon each individual spiritual gift, I want to impress upon you that you have one or more of the above gifts that may be lying dormant in your spirit. You may be using one of these gifts in a way that is blessing people already. You may be shying away from fully activating one of these gifts for fear of what others might think or missing opportunities (or blessings) because you have not said YES to utilizing your spiritual gifts. Your purpose may be on pause because you have not pressed play on your spiritual gifts. So please anchor into this truth. Your purpose is the path and the destination, but you cannot reach your destination without the vehicles of spiritual gifts. It's going to be the use of your spiritual gifts that allows your purpose to unfold and for you to arrive at your final divine destination. If you want your dreams to come true and desire to live out your purpose, you must pick up the phone and say yes to YOUR calling.

What do spiritual gifts have to do with your calling and living out your purpose? The calling or divine assignment for your life already exists within you. There may have been times when you felt a nudge, a hunch, or a push inside that demanded you pay attention to it. There may have been other times in your life when situations, events or even a voice is so loud you cannot ignore it. God is always speaking to you. Just like when a cell phone is on vibrate, it doesn't ring loud and clear, but you know someone is calling. Pay attention to the spiritual vibrations you feel on a daily basis. It's those unexplained gut feelings, the voice inside, that says go for it or take the next step. Those are examples of God's call on vibrate. God also knows that you may need a louder message sometimes, so He will put people in your path to directly communicate His message to you. He will cause abrupt things to happen to wake you up and move you into a new direction. He may even speak loud enough in your ear or in your spirit that you KNOW it's Him speaking to you. That's God's call with His unique ringtone on full blast.

PRESSED INTO MY PURPOSE

God has not forsaken you. He has not forgotten about you, and He won't leave you. He is speaking to you in every moment and situation you experience. The problem isn't that God doesn't hear you; the problem is more often that you do not *hear* Him because you are not *listening* with your heart and soul. Your purpose *is* your calling, and if you don't hear and answer YOUR call, you will *not* live out your purpose fully. Don't worry about taking every step towards your purpose perfectly. Just keep on taking destiny steps because God's promise is that He will be with you every step of the way up until you take your last breath. God will not abort you or your purpose. He's already given you permission to walk in your purpose and have what you want to have. Those dreams and desires deep down in your soul already have your name on them. God's just waiting for you to possess them. And through glorifying God and using your spiritual gifts to serve the world with love, He promises to give you the desires of your heart.

Once you say yes to your calling and start living with purpose, the next step is to serve *with* a purpose. Just as God has a vision, a plan, and purpose for your life, He also requires that your work in the world to be a ministry of service which does not mean you have to take on a role within a church or serve others in a physical building. Ministry simply means service to

God and other people in His name. Your ministry of service can be using your voice and gift of song in the choir to exhort and heal people or using your gift of wisdom to mentor young adults. Ministries are not confined to four walls, and there are no limitations on what your ministry can do for others. When you minister to others, you serve them with humility, love and compassion through your devotion to God. The sole intention of ministry is to treat and serve people like Jesus would.

I've answered my call and am using my spiritual gifts of shepherding, leadership, teaching, and wisdom as pastor of my church. All that I've experienced in my life has prepared and positioned me for THIS moment. When I arrived at The New Life Christian Center, I knew deep in my soul that I was home. Proverbs 18:16 says, "A man's gift maketh room for him, and bringeth him before great men." My spiritual gifts made room for me, and God has put me in the position to lead His people, but I cannot do it alone. Destiny is not a solo act. No one fulfills their purpose alone. I am so grateful for the team that God has put in place for me effectively carry out *His* vision. I feel so blessed, and I'm filled with joy as I carry out my purpose. God has been my rock in my times of trouble. The journey has not been easy or perfect, but I'm here!

PRESSED INTO MY PURPOSE

I am grateful for my natural and spiritual family, especially Oscar, my husband of forty plus years. He, too, is living his purpose and serving in his unique ministry. He also is a leader of a church and uses his spiritual gifts to serve the world. Oscar has been a strong tower of strength for me, and we are a strong team for God together.

I truly thank God for the *pressing*, for without it, I would not be the diamond I am today. When I wanted to give up on myself God refused to give up on me. Because of His love, mercy, and grace, I am here today sharing with you my purpose journey. If you feel uncertain about your purpose, don't give up because God won't give up you, either. He has the same love, mercy, and grace for you that He does for me. You are God's diamond, and the pressing you are experiencing right now is polishing you up for your shining purpose in the world.

If you don't digest anything I've written so far, digest this: Your purpose for living and being here is to glorify God and use your spiritual gifts in ministry to be of service to God's people. *How* you do that will not look like anyone else's purpose. God does not do encores! Once He created you, the mold was broken. Your purpose cannot be duplicated. You, my friend, are hand-crafted, designer's original. Therefore, you cannot compare what's happening in your life to what's happening in someone else's life. It is a total waste of energy to want what someone else has or to desire to be like someone else. God's purpose for your life cannot be imitated, and you cannot imitate the purpose that was given to another. If you are struggling in life right now, I challenge you to consider whether you are creating the chaos because you are resisting your purpose. I challenge you to consider whether the struggle is the result of you allowing your spiritual gifts to lie dormant.

I challenge you to consider whether the pain, suffering, or lack of deep fulfillment in your life is because you have not answered your call. I'm not saying that when you say yes to your purpose, answer the call, and utilize your spiritual gifts that life will be easy and drama free, though I am saying that your path will become clearer, more obstacles will be removed, favor will begin to fall upon you, doors will open up, opportunities will be presented to you, and you will begin to experience deep, satisfying joy.

Do you know your purpose? Have you answered YOUR call? Are you using your spiritual gifts to glorify and exalt God? If you have the gift of song, sing for God. If you are a wordsmith, use your words to glorify God. If you are a great teacher, teach the word of God.

If you are a compassionate caretaker, take care of God's people. If you know how to turn ideas into income, do that work in the church or for God's people. Whatever your gifts are, use them to build the kingdom of God and when you do, God will allow you to bear fruit and give you the desires of your heart. Stop waiting on God to open a door. Start walking in your purpose and using your spiritual gifts for God and the doors will open. Stop waiting on God to deliver you. Read His word, believe that you are already delivered, and put your faith in action to step out of bondage. Stop waiting for God to give you a good job. Start using your gifts to serve God's people, and He will give you the job you've been dreaming of. You are not waiting on God, He is waiting for you to answer the call, step into your purpose and activate your spiritual gifts.

God's already given you permission to serve with your gifts. You don't need a church to preach in, minister in the parking lot if you have to. You don't need a fancy house to gather people in need. Meet them in a coffee shop. You don't need a lot of money to get an education to counsel people. Show your love and compassion for a lost soul over the telephone. Stop making excuses for why you cannot do what you were created to do. Don't focus on the haters in your life, you're always going to have them; instead surround yourself with those who believe in you and keep taking your destiny steps. Stir up the gifts inside of you, activate them and just do it! Do what you were created to do without seeking the permission or approval of others. God's already given you the permission slip. Trust God in all things because He sees the end from the beginning. He already knows your journey and your final destination.

There is absolutely no excuse for you to NOT be living your purpose. You don't have to go on a mystical journey to find your purpose because it's been with you all along. You don't have to have a special gift to hear God's instructions for your life; you just have to listen. You don't need to necessarily go get an education to work your ministry either. You can start working it right now. You don't have to prove anything to God. You are already worthy of His love and favor.

Activate your purpose today by asking God to speak it to you, to show it to you, and lead you on the right path to fulfilling your purpose. Tell God that you are ready to answer His call. Ask God to reveal what your spiritual gifts are and to strengthen your faith as you serve the world. All you have is now because tomorrow is not promised. Say yes to your purpose and watch your life transform before your eyes. Start serving from your heart and see how your own life begins to evolve into the life of your dreams. Answer YOUR call and activate *your* purpose!

⌘ *Reflecting On My Purpose*

When my outer circumstances clearly illustrated that I couldn't trust God, I knew better and trusted Him anyway. I readily accepted my calling and my life changed for the better immediately. Every part of my life—spiritual, physical, emotional and financial—dramatically improved when I was obedient to God's command. I no longer felt intimidated by dyslexia or the world and became empowered with my spiritual gifts, knowledge, wisdom and the faith to do all things through Christ who strengthens me.

"Wherefore I put thee in remembrance that thou stir up the gift of God, which is in thee by the putting on of my hands." - ***2 Timothy 1:6***

⌘ *Time to Ponder Your Purpose*

What are you waiting for? What's keeping you from living your purpose? In life you can have excuses (reasons, rationale, and justifications) or results. What excuses have you been making that's keeping you from living in and walking out your purpose? What will you commit to doing right now to answer your call and activate your spiritual gifts? You are not here to settle; you are here to serve and succeed! You ARE God's diamond!

_____

_____

_____

_____

_____

_____

_____

_____

_____

CHAPTER 9

Making Room for Your Purpose

"If you wish to achieve worthwhile things in your personal and career life, you must become a worthwhile person in your own self-development."
– Brian Tracy

Your purpose is the path to your divine destiny, and in order to arrive at the place God envisions for you, you're going to need the "right" vessel and a vehicle to get you there. Living out your purpose will be like running a marathon instead of a quick sprint. You've got to get your mind, body and spirit ready for the long journey. I'm sure sprint runners put a lot of preparation, work, and training into the task of running that quick race. However, marathon runners begin training and preparing days, months, and even years before the extensive journey begins. Running a marathon requires you to get your mind, body and spirit into optimal shape in order to complete the task and come out victorious.

God will only fill you up to your current capacity. In other words, He will not give you what you are not ready to receive. If you are a pint-size person in spirit (your vessel), God will not pour a gallon of His blessings into you because you do not yet possess the capacity to carry the blessing. God knows that if He pours a gallon of His blessings into your pint-size spirit, more than three fourths of the blessing will overflow out of your vessel thus be "wasted." This does not mean you are not deserving of God's gallon-sized blessing; it simply means you are not spiritually, emotionally, physically, and even financially ready to possess and carry it. And truthfully, you will not know what to do with it. If you've been praying and asking God to give you big dreams, big amounts of money, impact, and territory and it hasn't happened yet, know that God hears your requests, but also knows you are not ready to receive it. Your vessel must be stretched into the capacity of that which you desire.

That means you have to begin doing some internal work to first remove the junk and clutter that is taking up valuable space. God loves you, but He will not plant good seed in "bad" soil because He knows those seeds will not flourish. God will not give you more than He knows you can handle. If your dreams, goals, and desires have not actualized yet or are not fruitful, you must check your soil (soul). Is your soul (spirit) cluttered with past hurts, bitterness, resentment, old wounds, grudges, or fear? Are you blaming others for your current circumstances? Are you failing to forgive yourself for past mistakes or others for the pain they've caused you? If you've answered yes to any of those questions, your vessel is filled with unfruitful seeds. Those seeds have turned into weeds called suffering, cynicism, worry, pessimism, distrust, anger, sadness, and blame. With that kind of soil and unfruitful weeds growing in your vessel, there is no room for God to pour in all the joy desire. You've got to start weeding your inner garden in order to produce the bounty of blessings you desire.

Weeds have no redeeming value relating to nutrition, food, or medicine. Some weeds are poisonous, they steal the nutrients from the soil, take up space, many leave seeds that reproduce, and they often have thorns and attract detrimental bugs. Weeds compete with plants that bear flowers or fruit by fighting to consume nutrients in the soil, water, and sunlight, leaving those plants starving for what they need to survive. If weeds are left intact, the neighboring flower or fruit-bearing plants can die or ill-produce. I'll tell you why this is important. As I previously stated, your spirit and soul is the soil of your garden. If your soil (soul/spirit) is full of weeds (pain, misery, shame, blame, anger, etc.), they will fight you internally for survival. Negative feelings and unresolved issues (weeds) will steal the nutrients (love, peace, joy, passion, purpose, dreams, etc.) from your soil and leave seeds behind (resentment, bitterness, and grudges) that will reproduce and stunt your growth (personal development, dreams, desires, and goals) or kill your spirit. Weeds are not just annoying plants, they are lethal to your survival, growth and reproduction.

Weeding your soul garden is necessary in order to completely cultivate your purpose. If you want God to pour out supernatural gallon-sized blessings, you need to expand your vessel to gallon-size capacity by making room for your purpose. Don't be ashamed of your weeds, everyone has them. Let's examine how many weeds (emotional and spiritual clutter) you have and then discuss how you can begin to expand your capacity to receive all you desire. Review the statements below and put a check mark by the ones that are true for you right now. This is not a scientific test, and there are no right or wrong answers. Don't try to "look good" when you respond because, if you do, you are not helping yourself; you are hindering the opportunity to truly identify the weeds keeping you stuck or stagnant in life. Be honest, no one will see this but you.

DR. LORRAINE CHATMON

How Many Weeds Are Growing in Your Soul Garden?

___ I am frequently agitated or irritable.

___ It doesn't take much to make me angry.

___ People can easily get on my nerves.

___ I am often impatient.

___ I get frustrated easily.

___ It's easy for me to find fault in others.

___ I tend to compare myself (my looks, my possessions, my family, my income level, etc.) to other people I know.

___ I have a hard time letting go of the grudges I hold.

___ There are people I haven't forgiven yet.

___ I have the tendency to be envious and jealous of others.

___ I'm still blaming people for their past mistakes.

___ I haven't forgiven myself for mistakes I've made in the past.

___ I tend to procrastinate when it comes to accomplishing my goals.

PRESSED INTO MY PURPOSE

___ I'm more pessimistic than I am optimistic.

___ I often second-guess my decisions and choices.

___ I feel ashamed about things I've done in the past.

___ I can be quite suspicious of other people's intentions.

___ Sometimes I feel sad inside, but don't know why.

___ I seem to have more excuses than I do results.

___ I don't feel like I have clear directions for what my Next steps are.

___ I have a hard time believing in things I cannot see.

Out of the twenty statements, how many are true for you right now? I want you to re-examine the statements you selected and ask yourself why the statement is true for you? Don't settle for an "I don't know" answer. Keep asking "why" for each one and then write down your responses. It doesn't matter if three or fifteen are true for you. Identify them, ask yourself why, look closely at your responses, and you'll discover that you have a deeply rooted pain or trauma (bad or negative life experience) attached to each one of them. Discovering your deeply rooted pains does not necessarily mean you are fatally flawed or that you need to seek counseling or therapy, although it can be helpful. The purpose of this exercise is to give you just a glimpse into what you might be carrying around in your vessel that's preventing you from being filled with your purpose.

Carrying out God's purpose for your life is a sacred gift, and God wants you to make room for Him to pour into you. It's your responsibility to care for your vessel. What are you going to do to extract the emotional weeds from your life? You only have two choices: You can continue to hoard them and hinder your purpose, or you can heal from them and allow in more peace, joy, fulfillment, gratitude and optimism.

Here are Seven Strategies to Expand the Capacity of Your Soul

1. **Become saved.** If you have not already, ask God to come into your life and accept Jesus Christ as your personal savior. It's that simple. Tell God you are ready to be saved. State and acknowledge that you know Christ died on the cross for your sins and that you accept Him as your personal savior.

2. **Dedicate time towards cultivating your purpose every day.** Ask God to show you your

purpose. Ask Him to reveal it clearly and guide your next steps. Read your Bible and meditate on the word. Get a Biblical concordance or a Bible that helps you understand the scriptures. Attend Bible school or Bible study groups. Connect with and surround yourself with people who are already living on purpose. Create opportunities to use your spiritual gifts on a daily basis. Create a purpose vision board and reflect upon it every day. Create a plan for carrying out your purpose and execute it. Keep a gratitude journal and document all the things you are grateful for. Spend your time doing things that you are passionate about.

3. **Tell yourself the truth about the current conditions of your soil (soul).** Stop lying to yourself about what's going on in your life and step out of any denial that your spirit may be suffering from old wounds, pain, and/or negative life experiences. The truth really does set you free. You don't have to announce it to the world or share the truth with anyone else, but you must express the truth to begin uprooting the weeds.

4. **Make a daily commitment to weeding your garden.** You can't just pluck the weeds from the

surface, you've got to extract the deep seated roots for long-lasting healing and transformation. Forms of deep extraction may include participating in individual or group counseling, seeking the support of a mentor, or seeking spiritual counsel. Distance yourself from toxic people who belittle you, cause stress in your life, and don't support you. When you begin to live on purpose, you will lose people or ask them to leave. Either way, you are expanding the capacity to allow in healthy people and relationships.

5. **Forgive those who've hurt you.** *Real* forgiveness happens when the thought of the person who hurt you and how they hurt you no longer consumes your spirit, makes you angry, or causes you to behave in unhealthy ways. While you may never forget what happened, it becomes a distant memory that no longer has power in your life. Real forgiveness is a gift to you and the person who hurt you. Failing to truly forgive holds you captive in your own skin. Holding on to grudges and pain shrinks the capacity of your vessel and blocks your blessings.

6. **Practice daily self-care.** Your body is God's temple! 1 Corinthians 6: 19-20 says, *"What? Know ye not that your body is the temple of the Holy Ghost which is in you, which ye have of God, and ye are not your own? For ye are bought with a price: therefore glorify God in your body, and in your spirit, which are God's."* Your body is the vehicle you'll need to live out your purpose. Just like a car, if you don't get an oil change, tune up, rotate the tires, and perform regular maintenance, the car will break down before you get all the mileage out of it or get to your destination. Put yourself first by getting adequate rest, feed your body healthy food (if God lives within your temple, why would you serve Him junk?), move your body and exercise, keep your appearance up, practice daily grooming, honor your body by keeping it free from toxins, drugs, alcohol, and other substances that can diminish your health. You only get ONE vehicle, and you need to be in optimum health for the long journey.

7. **Ignite your passions and do what you love.** There are two vital questions you must ask to find your passionate purpose. The first question is what are you passionate about? Passion is highly connected to your purpose. Where there

is passion, there is excitement and energy. Often, you will be in love with what you're passionate about and can't imagine not doing. However, it is possible to be passionate about something you are not good at or that you are not called to do. A perfect example would be someone who loves to sing, but does not have good tone or pitch. They may LOVE to sing, but they are not very good at it. What are you passionate about? Get out of your comfort zone and try the things you've been dreaming of. They just may spark some excitement and passion that will not only lead you to your purpose, but expand your capacity to receive God's gallon-sized blessings. The second vital question to ask yourself is what your strengths are and what you're good at. What do you excel at? What do you do better than anyone you know? What comes very easy and naturally to you? What activities do you participate in that you could get lost in? Pay attention to the things that excite you, fire you up, and make you feel good and those that you could do all day without getting tired or becoming weary. When you are living in your strengths, you feel empowered and energized. Once you discover what you are passionate about and what you love, do it as often as you can and share your passion with other people to bless their lives.

To simplify the whole mystery, keep these two factors in mind. Your greatest purpose in life is to know and have a relationship with God and to discover your spiritual gifts and use them to serve the world as an act of love. If you can do this, you are living on purpose. Keep this in mind and don't overcomplicate the act of living out your purpose. God says your gifts will make room for you, but you must first make room for God, your gifts, and your purpose by expanding the capacity of your vessel. God is ready to pour out His blessings, and He wants to give you more than you can ever imagine. God is waiting for you to pull those weeds and re-fertilize your soil so you can bear His fruit and flourish.

Now that you have spent time examining your soul and weeding your garden, I hope you've discovered that suffering, low self-esteem, bitterness, anger, hate and jealousy are cluttering up your capacity to possess your great purpose. The process of de-cluttering your life is just like spring cleaning. Have you ever spent a day deep cleaning your house and stumbled upon hidden or forgotten treasures such as books you love, photos that make you smile, or sentimental trinkets you forgot you had? When you spring clean your soul, the same experience is true. You begin to remember what makes your heart smile, you find your passion again, and you reveal your gifts. Spring cleaning and soul weeding is not a one-time event. You must commit to keeping your vessel, your purpose container, empty of garbage so it can be filled with dreams, desires, goals, ideas, passions, and God's purpose for your life.

Once you discover your purpose, don't stop there. You need to make room daily for more of God's blessings to be poured into you. I challenge you to wake up every day and say, "God, I am NOT full yet. I'm still hungry. Feed me. Pour into me until your blessings overflow." No doubt He will hear you and respond. Let God know you are ready to receive more of His love, grace, mercy, and favor. Invite God in to impregnate your spirit with ideas, dreams, goals, and desires that will allow you to use your spiritual gifts to be of service to God's people. Be mindful that the pouring out of His blessings does not need to be grand, they can be small powerful drops of divine direction. This is where many believers get it wrong. Mother Theresa did not drive a Bentley, she was not a millionaire, nor did she live in an eight bedroom mansion. She was a simple woman who loved ministering to and caring for the poor. She was quite comfortable in low places, non-ideal circumstances, and felt most inspired by mingling with the homeless and hopeless. God uses ordinary people to do extraordinary things!

Are you ready to be like Mary, the mother of Jesus? Mary is a perfect example of ordinary people being chosen to do extraordinary things. While you may not be chosen to birth the son of God, what you are to become impregnated with is still very significant in God's eyes. You can learn a lot from Mary's story and her obedience to God's calling on her life. Mary was imperfect just like you and I, but her vessel had been cultivated to carry the most important purpose ever. As you continue to examine your vessel, keep these lessons from Mary in mind.

- Mary was undoubtedly aligned with God, her spiritual purpose partner. Mary was a believer. She communed with God daily and believed in miracles. She was always connected to her spiritual lifeline and chose to show reverence of God's presence and power.

- Mary was spiritually available. Her soul and spirit were open to receive. Her heart was pure, and it wasn't cluttered with chaos, junk, and weeds. She kept her vessel clear and free from things that would block the blessings God would pour into her.

- Mary was a YES woman! She was spiritually, emotionally and physically willing to allow God to do a great thing within her and to use her for greater glory. Though afraid, she trusted God even when she did not have all the answers or understood exactly why she was chosen to birth the Son of God.

- Mary had a humble spirit. She did not boast about carrying the Son of God. She was quiet in her purpose, and her faith and belief was unwavering. When Jesus was born, Mary did not run around telling the world about its greatest gift. She allowed the gift (Jesus) to speak for itself and remained humbled and faithful to her purpose.

- Mary expected miracles, even in the face of grave disappointments and tragedy. Mary never doubted. She believed with unshakable faith that God would do what He promised and that He would finish what He started. Mary was steadfast, relentless, and resilient as she trusted God's word, no matter what the circumstances looked like. She believed in God's promises, did not faint, and was faithful until she took her last breath.

You, too, can be like Mary. Whether you deem your purpose "big or small," you must be aligned with God, your spiritual purpose partner. You must be spiritually available and say yes to your purpose. You must be humble, faithful, have unwavering belief, and trust that God is going to perform miracles in your life every day. Another important aspect of Mary's purpose is that she found it and lost herself in it. That is exactly what God expects you to do. He wants you to discover your purpose, live it, and become lost in the divinity of His glory. When you become lost in your purpose, it no longer is about you. Here's how you can tell if you've become lost in your purpose.

Signs that you are losing yourself in your purpose.

1. You know your purpose is too big to do alone.

2. You begin to feel like you need a team to accomplish your purpose.

3. You know that what you are doing needs to make a difference.

4. You begin to feel overwhelmed with the purpose and need others to make it a reality.

5. You feel a sense of urgency to accomplish your mission.

6. You move from being successful to becoming significant.

7. You get bored with your career and crave more of a calling.

Losing yourself in your purpose delights the Lord. Living out your purpose is not about you. Your purpose may be to help someone else fulfill their purpose. Your purpose and role in life may be for you to not be the leading actor, but to be best supporting actor/actress. Maybe your purpose is to add value to the purpose or dream of another. God is all-knowing and He does not make mistakes. Don't doubt His wisdom if your purpose is to be of support to another person's purpose. Don't make it (your purpose) about you. Your purpose is God's plan. Say yes to His plan and He will pave the way, protect you, give you the desires of your heart, and you will prosper. God's waiting to pour out His purpose into your vessel. Don't delay; start making room for your purpose today.

> *"For I know the thoughts that I think toward you, saith the LORD, thoughts of peace, and not of evil, to give you an expected end."*
> **-Jeremiah 29:11**

⌘ *Reflecting On My Purpose*

I believe I have the seeds of greatness and empowerment within me. I now acknowledge that I am open to attract others into my life, for which I will evolve and therefore harvest. And with this, I've now decided to be both a student and a teacher. I now surrender my human will to the divine will of God and trust that HE will lead me on this journey called LIFE! Now that the dust has settled, I'm ready to rise and shine! I am a new creature, old things have passed away, and behold, I am new. I am ready to put the sparkle in my purpose with glitz and glam. Why? Because I AM a daughter of the king. I AM God's diamond!

⌘ *Time To Ponder Your Purpose*

Imagine who you can become, what you can have and experience, and what you can do when you make room for your purpose. Take a moment and write down your wildest dreams, hopes, wishes, plans, and desires. Get creative, have fun, think big, and believe that NOTHING is impossible for God. What will your life be like when you say yes to your purpose, make room for it, and live it fully?

_____

_____

_____

_____

_____

_____

_____

_____

_____

CHAPTER 10

It's Time to Shine

"The question isn't who is going to let me. It's who is going to stop me." – Ayn Rand

Dyslexia did not steal or sabotage my dreams, nor did doubt, distractions, delays, or detours derail my destiny! I did it! I AM living out my purpose. The scared and ashamed little girl who once existed no longer lives. The roots of her existence have been plucked from my spirit. She served a purpose in the grand scheme of God's plan, yet her role has expired. Isn't God amazing? God *never* aborts His promises and He *always* finishes what He starts. My vessel and vehicle has brought me a mighty long way, and I am grateful.

My purpose is still unfolding before my eyes, and I am just as eager to fulfill my destiny as I was when I was a shiny-eyed twenty year old. As I enter my golden years, I realize how important it is to shine and that it's never too late to shine.

PRESSED INTO MY PURPOSE

I'm in my sixties, and you better believe I am getting my shine on because my God created me to. I have no intentions on letting age stop my brilliance!

It's your time to shine! You don't have to wait until you reach a certain point in your destiny; you can shine right now. Because when God created you, he poured salt and light into your spirit. I understand that sometimes life's circumstances may seem dark and that you may want to hide in the shadows, but I'm daring you to step out from behind those shadows and shine anyway! You were not created to be dim, dull, and dark. You were born a jewel in God's treasure chest, and He intended for you to shine when you took your first breath up until you take your last breath. Scripture says, "Ye are the salt of the earth: but if the salt have lost his flavor, wherewith shall it be salted? It is thenceforth good for nothing, but to be cast out, and to be trodden under foot of men. Ye are the light of the world. A city that is set on a hill cannot be hid. Neither do men light a candle, and put it under a bushel, but on a candlestick; and it giveth light unto all that are in the house.

Let your light so shine before men, that they may see your good works, and glorify your Father which is in heaven," (Matthew 5:13-16). It's time to share your salt (spiritual gifts) and light (purpose) with the world.

It's time to toss out the old to make room the newness that God has for you. The Bible speaks of the renewing of your mind. Scripture encourages us to have the belief that we can change old habits and thoughts and create new ones. When you hold on to the old, you allow past experiences to leave a toxic residue in your spirit that eventually creates a build-up that blocks your blessings. When you stay stuck in the past, you paralyze the progress of your purpose. I challenge you today to stop the obsession about things and people of the past. Let it go! Let them go! It's time for you to shine brightly from the inside out like a city on a hill. Have you ever met someone who seemed to just light up the room with their presence? What you are experiencing is the witnessing of God in them. Behind the scenes, they may not have it all together, but they know who their creator is and they believe in God's promise for them. They've made a conscious decision to shine on the inside, regardless of what their outer circumstances may look like. I just love it when I see someone walking in their own brilliance because it inspires me to do the same.

There is no shame in shining! To give forth a glow of light and to be bright is what it means to shine. Many of God's people are wandering in the dark—lost, lonely, hurt and confused. They are desperately seeking to find direction in their life. They truly want to escape the darkness they are in and are in need of finding even a glimpse of light to continue to carry on. Many people are facing turbulent situations in their life and may be losing hope. They are seeking the light. They are seeking God. They are seeking *you* because God is in you and light is in God. When you choose to shine your light, you become that city on a hill. You become a lighthouse ushering the lost ones to shore. Your light is not just for you. Your light was especially created for you to guide people back to God to the shores of safety. God knew what He was doing when He gave us light. He knew there would be people who needed our specific light to return to the Kingdom. When you are feeling like it's selfish to shine, just remember you were created to shine. God expects you to shine for *His* glory!

Life may be pressing you right now, but I want you to just lean in to that press and tell God to press on! I want you to look at your current circumstances and laugh out loud at them. I want you to push back when life starts pressing you. With every push, you are creating your own unique cut, color, and shape of your purpose diamond. Do you realize how much of a co-creator you are with God? You don't have to do anything alone. God is always holding out His hand, waiting for you to take it so you two can create supernatural miracles together. He's always been there for you, and He will not leave or forsake you. I challenge you to shift your perspective and way of thinking to that of a co-creator instead of a victim, lone ranger, or helpless bystander. You were created with greatness within you and you are a champion. Today is the day you suit up and enter the battlefield to fight for your purpose. You are a gladiator, and you *will* win with God fighting right next to you. Nothing will stop you because you are unstoppable!

Your choices definitely determine your circumstances. In every second of the day, you make choices. The choices you've made up until this point in your life have brought you to right where you are in your life. There's no benefit in blaming other people for where you are in life. Things happened to you, but they do not have to become *who* you are. We've all been on the receiving end of pain, hurt, or abuse, but you've got to exercise the courage to shake it loose, shake it off, and release the pain from your life.

Starting today, I want you to stop blaming people, including yourself, for where you are, who you are, and what you have. Instead, I want you to commit to making purpose-driven choices every day from this day forward.

Here's a few examples of what purpose-driven choices look like:

PRESSED INTO MY PURPOSE

- *I will trust and believe in God at all times.*
- *I will stand in my power instead of being paralyzed.*
- *I will live my purpose, no matter what.*
- *I will use my spiritual gifts to serve God's people.*
- *I will live with passion and do only what I love.*
- *I will believe instead of doubt.*
- *I will take action instead of waiting.*
- *I will trust my genius instead of comparing myself to others.*
- *I will listen to and obey the commands of God.*
- *I will see possibilities instead of problems.*
- *I will be powerful instead of pitiful.*
- *I will exercise my faith instead of being fearful.*
- *I will forgive instead of holding grudges.*
- *I will see the greatness in others instead of gossiping about them.*

These are just a few purpose-driven choices you can make every day. When you go through your day making these kinds of choices, you will create the life you desire, live on purpose, and be in alignment with God's will for your life. I won't promise you that every moment or every day will be perfect, peaceful, or filled with pleasure, but just remember when life presses you down, you push back. The pressing is not designed to paralyze you, it's divinely created to *press you into your purpose*.

You are perfectly and fabulously flawed, just like a diamond is supposed to be. Everything about you is unique. There is no other jewel in God's treasure chest like you. He handcrafted you to be who you are and to carry out a purposeful assignment that no one can carry out but you. You've been called to do great things in the world and to make a meaningful difference in the lives of others. Discovering and living out your purpose will help you accomplish that mission. You already have everything you need within to make it to the mountaintop. Yes, you are going to have to do more work, master your craft, and polish your skills for the journey. That may require you to get a mentor, participate in personal and professional coaching, get additional training and education, and continuously work on becoming your best self from the inside out. While you are working on you, be expectant that God will be working in and through you.

Let's recap the power points of purpose I've shared thus far so you can get to work and start walking in your purpose! What I've presented to you of course is not everything to consider, but the information will get you well on your way to purposeful greatness!

Below I've shared one of the most important and powerful points about living your purpose from each chapter. I want you to ponder on the purpose points and then write down at least one action you are ready to take right now to discover, embrace, and live out your purpose.

CHAPTER 1

How will you use your life experiences to take the next step in living on purpose?

_____

_____

CHAPTER 2

Let go of those old labels! Redefine who you are in the eyes of God.

_____

_____

CHAPTER 3

Be purpose driven! What new possibilities do you now see?

_____

_____

CHAPTER 4

Your destiny awaits! Who can you align yourself with? Identify your new destiny seekers!

_____

_____

CHAPTER 5

It's time to connect the dots! What has God been preparing you for? Where is the pressing in your life leading you?

_____

_____

CHAPTER 6

How will you begin to follow God's will for your life and use your free will wisely?

_____

_____

CHAPTER 7

Your relationship with God is your highest priority. How will you strengthen it?

_____

_____

CHAPTER 8

No more excuses! What results do you want to experience within the next 30 days?

_____

_____

CHAPTER 9

It's time to live on purpose! Which wildest dreams will you make come true within the next 30 days?

_____

_____

CHAPTER 10

You are God's diamond! In what unique ways do (and will) you shine?

_____

_____

The most powerful act you can commit right now is to exercise your "free will" according to God's will for your life. When obedience and destiny collide, miracles begin to happen suddenly, frequently and abundantly! Wouldn't you love to have God bless you with miracles right when you need them, as often as you need them, and as many as you need? You CAN have it all when you say yes to your purpose, answer your call, and make purpose-driven choices in every moment. God is ready to bless you in ways you can only imagine. He's waiting on you, but you can't expect the blessings without some pressing!

All of my pain, problems, challenges, and suffering have made me the woman I am today. I've gained wisdom from my wounds, calm from the chaos, power from my problems, and clarity and confidence from my challenges. While I was going through it, I wanted to quit and give up, but I am so grateful God kept whispering keep the faith and that He gave me the strength to take steps in the dark.

Every disappointment, setback, financial struggle, hurt, and challenge pressed me until I thought the life would be pressed out of me. I was cut, shaped, sharpened, and polished through it all. Today, I can say I don't regret any of what I went through. I am grateful to be able to share my story with you in hopes to encourage and inspire you to keep pressing on through the pressing moments. You, too, are being pressed into YOUR purpose!

God is shaping and molding you into the masterpiece He envisions. Believe me, He knows exactly what He is doing. Trust Him. Lean in and be flexible with what you are experiencing right now.

Let the following passage encourage your heart today, and reflect upon it often on your purpose journey.

Ecclesiastes 3:1-14 King James Version (KJV)

To every-thing there is a season, and a time to every purpose under the heavens:

A time to be born, and a time to die; a time to plant, and a time to pluck up that which is planted;

A time to kill, and a time to heal; a time to break down, and a time to build up;

A time to weep, and a time to laugh; a time to mourn, and a time to dance;

A time to cast away stones, and a time to gather stones together; a time to embrace, and a time to refrain from embracing;

A time to get, and a time to lose; a time to keep, and a time to cast away;

A time to rend, and a time to sew; a time to keep silence, and a time to speak;

A time to love, and a time to hate; a time of war, and a time of peace.

What profit hath he that worketh in that wherein he laboureth?

I have seen the travail, which God hath given to the sons of men to be exercised in it.

> *He hath made everything beautiful in his time: also he hath set the world in their heart, so that no man can find out the work that God maketh from the beginning to the end.*
>
> *I know that there is no good in them, but for a man to rejoice, and to do good in his life.*
>
> *And also that every man should eat and drink, and enjoy the good of all his labour, it is the gift of God.*
>
> *I know that, whatsoever God doeth, it shall be forever: nothing can be put to it, nor anything taken from it: and God doeth it, that men should fear before him.*

It doesn't matter what season in life you are in right now. It doesn't matter if your current circumstances don't appear to be favorable—whether you are in transition, doing great in life, or feel like you've already arrived. God is the creator of seasons and He knows we all have our moments and that there is a time for everything.

Regardless of where you stand in your purpose journey, there is more and better waiting for you to experience. God has an unlimited source of health, wealth, love, joy, peace, happiness, fulfillment and prosperity ready to be poured into you.

God sees the end and it's beautiful. He chose you. He created you. You are God's diamond! He has great plans for your life. Your purpose is coming to pass right now in THIS season of your life. Invite God into your life. Strengthen your relationship with Him. Answer YOUR call. Expand your vessel and stretch your capacity to receive all His goodness, blessings and miracles. Trust the ebbs and flow, no matter what. Believe and be faithful.

THIS is your season! Say yes to your purpose and don't resist the press! You are God's diamond, all ready to shine! Shine on... shine on!

⌘ *Reflecting On My Purpose*

My purpose has nothing to do with money, houses, cars, or land. I AM here to love. I am here to lead, encourage and inspire. I am here to heal and counsel. I AM here because He chose me to be great and to do extraordinary things. I'm living in and on purpose, and it feels spectacular. I am free and empowered. I am called, and I say yes every day to my purpose. I AM God's diamond and so are YOU. Shine bright!

⌘ *Time To Ponder Your Purpose*

Take time to write down the deepest desires of your heart. What's the vision for your life? How would you like to use your spiritual gifts? What miracles would you like to see happen in your life? Get bold and creative. Make your declarations known to God today. When God shows up and shows out in your life, what will it look like? Once you create your purposeful vision, get busy co-creating with God and then go out into the world and be that city on a hill and serve with love to glorify God!

_____

_____

_____

_____

_____

_____

_____

_____

AFTERWORD

Scriptures for Your Purpose Journey

Refer to these scriptures when you are feeling lost, afraid, unsure, or doubtful on your journey to living a purpose-driven life.

Psalms 138:8
The Lord will fulfill his purpose for me; your steadfast love, O Lord, endures forever. Do not forsake the work of your hands.

Romans 12:2 ESV
Do not be conformed to this world, but be transformed by the renewal of your mind, that by testing, you may discern what is the will of God, what is good and acceptable and perfect.

Romans 8:28 ESV
And we know that for those who love God, all things work together for good, for those who are called according to his purpose.

Matthew 5:13-16 ESV
"You are the salt of the earth, but if salt has lost its taste, how shall its saltiness be restored? It is no longer good for anything except to be thrown out and

trampled under people's feet. "You are the light of the world. A city set on a hill cannot be hidden. Nor do people light a lamp and put it under a basket, but on a stand, and it gives light to all in the house. In the same way, let your light shine before others, so that they may see your good works and give glory to your Father who is in heaven.

Philippians 4:13 ESV
I can do all things through him who strengthens me.

Job 22:21 ESV
"Agree with God, and be at peace; thereby good will come to you".

Habakkuk 2:3 ESV
For still the vision awaits its appointed time; it hastens to the end -it will not lie. If it seems slow, wait for it; it will surely come; it will not delay.

Matthew 28:19-20 ESV
"Go, therefore, and make disciples of all nations, baptizing them in the name of the Father and of the Son and of the Holy Spirit, teaching them to observe all that I have commanded you. And behold, I am with you always, to the end of the age."

Matthew 6:33 ESV
But seek first the kingdom of God and his righteousness, and all these things will be added to you.

Jeremiah 1:5 ESV
"Before I formed you in the womb I knew you, and before you were born I consecrated you; I appointed you a prophet to the nations."

Romans 12:1-5
I appeal to you therefore, brothers, by the mercies of God, to present your bodies as a living sacrifice, holy and acceptable to God, which is your spiritual worship. Do not be conformed to this world, but be transformed by the renewal of your mind, that by testing you may discern what is the will of God, what is good and acceptable and perfect. For by the grace given to me, I say to everyone among you not to think of himself more highly than he ought to think, but to think with sober judgment, each according to the measure of faith that God has assigned. For as in one body we have many members, and the members do not all have the same function, so we, though many, are one body in Christ, and individually members one of another.

PRESSED INTO MY PURPOSE

Psalm 73:26
My flesh and my heart may fail, but God is the strength of my heart and my portion forever.

Ephesians 1:11
In him we have obtained an inheritance, having been predestined according to the purpose of him who works all things according to the counsel of his will.

Revelation 4:11 ESV
"Worthy are you, our Lord and God, to receive glory and honor and power, for you created all things, and by your will they existed and were created."

2 Corinthians 12:9-10 ESV
But he said to me, "My grace is sufficient for you, for my power is made perfect in weakness." Therefore, I will boast all the more gladly of my weaknesses, so that the power of Christ may rest upon me. For the sake of Christ, then, I am content with weaknesses, insults, hardships, persecutions, and calamities. For when I am weak, then I am strong.

Psalm 57:2 ESV
I cry out to God Most High, to God who fulfills his purpose for me.

1 Corinthians 6:19-20 ESV

Or do you not know that your body is a temple of the Holy Spirit within you, whom you have from God? You are not your own, for you were bought with a price. So glorify God in your body.

Ezra 10:4

Arise, for it is your task, and we are with you; be strong and do it."

Galatians 1:15 ESV

But when he who had set me apart before I was born, and who called me by his grace...

Ecclesiastes 12:13-14 ESV

The end of the matter; all has been heard. Fear God and keep his commandments, for this is the whole duty of man. For God will bring every deed into judgment, with every secret thing, whether good or evil.

John 16:13 ESV

When the Spirit of truth comes, he will guide you into all the truth, for he will not speak on his own authority, but whatever he hears he will speak, and he will declare to you the things that are to come.

PRESSED INTO MY PURPOSE

Isaiah 55:11 ESV
So shall my word be that goes out from my mouth; it shall not return to me empty, but it shall accomplish that which I purpose, and shall succeed in the thing for which I sent it.

1 John 1:9 ESV
If we confess our sins, he is faithful and just to forgive us our sins and to cleanse us from all unrighteousness.

Colossians 3:23 ESV
Whatever you do, work heartily, as for the Lord and not for men.

2 Timothy 1:9 ESV
Who saved us and called us to a holy calling, not because of our works, but because of his own purpose and grace, which he gave us in Christ Jesus before the ages began...

John 5:30 ESV
I can do nothing on my own. As I hear, I judge, and my judgment is just, because I seek not my own will but the will of him who sent me.

Ephesians 2:10 ESV
For we are his workmanship, created in Christ Jesus for good works, which God prepared beforehand, that we should walk in them.

Matthew 16:25 ESV
For whoever would save his life will lose it, but whoever loses his life for my sake will find it.

Revelation 21:4 ESV
He will wipe away every tear from their eyes, and death shall be no more, neither shall there be mourning, nor crying, nor pain anymore, for the former things have passed away.

Psalm 8:6 ESV
You have given him dominion over the works of your hands; you have put all things under his feet.

Acts 1:8 ESV
But you will receive power when the Holy Spirit has come upon you, and you will be my witnesses in Jerusalem and in all Judea and Samaria, and to the end of the earth."

1 Corinthians 2:9-13 ESV
But, as it is written, "What no eye has seen, nor ear heard, nor the heart of man imagined, what God has prepared for those who love him"— these things God has revealed to us through the Spirit. For the Spirit searches everything, even the depths of God. For who knows a person's thoughts except the spirit of that person, which is in him? So also no one comprehends the thoughts of God except the Spirit of God. Now we have received not the spirit of the world, but the Spirit

who is from God, that we might understand the things freely given us by God. And we impart this in words not taught by human wisdom but taught by the Spirit, interpreting spiritual truths to those who are spiritual.

Psalm 100:1-5 ESV
A Psalm for giving thanks. Make a joyful noise to the Lord, all the earth! Serve the Lord with gladness! Come into his presence with singing! Know that the Lord, he is God! It is he who made us, and we are his; we are his people, and the sheep of his pasture. Enter his gates with thanksgiving, and his courts with praise! Give thanks to him; bless his name! For the Lord is good; his steadfast love endures forever, and his faithfulness to all generations.

Isaiah 46:10 ESV
Declaring the end from the beginning and from ancient times things not yet done, saying, "My counsel shall stand, and I will accomplish all my purpose,"

Ecclesiastes 12:13 ESV
The end of the matter; all has been heard. Fear God and keep his commandments, for this is the whole duty of man.

Romans 6:17 ESV
But thanks be to God, that you who were once slaves of sin have become obedient from the heart to the standard of teaching to which you were committed.

Isaiah 49:4 ESV
But I said, "I have labored in vain; I have spent my strength for nothing and vanity; yet surely my right is with the Lord, and my recompense with my God."

John 14:6 ESV
Jesus said to him, "I am the way, and the truth, and the life. No one comes to the Father except through me."

1 Corinthians 3:12-15 ESV
Now if anyone builds on the foundation with gold, silver, precious stones, wood, hay, straw, each one's work will become manifest, for the day will disclose it, because it will be revealed by fire, and the fire will test what sort of work each one has done. If the work that anyone has built on the foundation survives, he will receive a reward. If anyone's work is burned up, he will suffer loss, though he himself will be saved, but only as through fire.

Hebrews 12:1 ESV
Therefore, since we are surrounded by so great a cloud of witnesses, let us also lay aside every weight, and sin

which clings so closely, and let us run with endurance the race that is set before us.

James 1:1-27 ESV
James, a servant of God and of the Lord Jesus Christ, to the twelve tribes in the Dispersion: Greetings. Count it all joy, my brothers, when you meet trials of various kinds, for you know that the testing of your faith produces steadfastness. And let steadfastness have its full effect, that you may be perfect and complete, lacking in nothing. If any of you lacks wisdom, let him ask God, who gives generously to all without reproach, and it will be given him.

2 Timothy 2:14-15
Remind them of these things, and charge them before God not to quarrel about words, which does no good, but only ruins the hearers. Do your best to present yourself to God as one approved, a worker who has no need to be ashamed, rightly handling the word of truth.

Ephesians 2:1-10 ESV
And you were dead in the trespasses and sins in which you once walked, following the course of this world, following the prince of the power of the air, the spirit that is now at work in the sons of disobedience—among whom we all once lived in the passions of our

flesh, carrying out the desires of the body and the mind, and were by nature children of wrath, like the rest of mankind. But God, being rich in mercy, because of the great love with which he loved us, even when we were dead in our trespasses, made us alive together with Christ -by grace you have been save...

2 Corinthians 3:18 ESV
And we all, with unveiled face, beholding the glory of the Lord, are being transformed into the same image from one degree of glory to another. For this comes from the Lord who is the Spirit.

Psalm 23:1-6 ESV
A Psalm of David. The Lord is my shepherd; I shall not want. He makes me lie down in green pastures. He leads me beside still waters. He restores my soul. He leads me in paths of righteousness for his name's sake. Even though I walk through the valley of the shadow of death, I will fear no evil, for you are with me; your rod and your staff, they comfort me. You prepare a table before me in the presence of my enemies; you anoint my head with oil; my cup overflows...

Jeremiah 29:11-13 ESV
For I know the plans I have for you, declares the Lord, plans for welfare and not for evil, to give you a future and a hope. Then you will call upon me and come and

PRESSED INTO MY PURPOSE

pray to me, and I will hear you. You will seek me and find me, when you seek me with all your heart.

SOURCE:
openbible.info/topics/purpose_in_life

ABOUT THE AUTHOR

Dr. Lorraine Chatmon serves as Senior Pastor and teacher at New Life Christian Center Church in Emporia, Virginia. A native daughter of Emporia, she began her kingdom assignment as Co-Pastor at New Life Church and served faithfully for eight years before fulfilling her current title of Senior Pastor.

Dr. Chatmon has a plethora of educational experience, holding an Associate's Degree in Human Services from Southside Community College in Alberta, VA, a Bachelor's of Arts Degree in Organizational Management from St. Paul's College in Lawrenceville, VA, a Master's Degree in Christian Education from Berean Light Institute located in Emporia, VA, and a Doctoral Degree in Biblical Counseling from Andersonville

Theological Seminary in Virginia. Additionally, she completed coursework at Virginia State University in Petersburg, VA to become a certified nutritionist.

Dr. Chatmon is currently retired, living her purpose and pursuing other aspirations and dreams. Appointed by God and anointed by the Holy Ghost to preach a one-time, fiery message, Pastor Chatmon provides practical, yet insightful and powerful tools that empower people to become true disciples of Christ, equipped to live up to their fullest potential in God. Dedicated to spreading the good news of the Gospel, she is a sought after preacher, speaker, revivalist, lecturer, and worship leader, who is regularly called upon to encourage people of God.

To learn more, be sure to visit:

www.LorraineChatmon.com
www.BeautifulRichLife.com

WE WANT TO HEAR FROM YOU!!!

If this book has made a difference in your life Dr. Lorraine would be delighted to hear about it.

Leave a review on Amazon.com!

BOOK DR. LORRAINE TO SPEAK AT YOUR NEXT EVENT!

Send an email to booking@publishyourgift.com

Learn more about Dr. Lorraine at:
www.LorraineChatmon.com

"EMPOWERING YOU TO IMPACT GENERATIONS"
WWW.PUBLISHYOURGIFT.COM

www.ingramcontent.com/pod-product-compliance
Lightning Source LLC
Chambersburg PA
CBHW070106120526
44588CB00032B/1141